BURIED IN MY HEART

A TRUE LOVE STORY

SARA LEPTIS

Publish Authority

Buried in My Heart
A Story of Love in War-torn Lydia

All events, locales, conversations, and observations in this book are from the author's memories of them, from her perspective. In some cases, names of individuals, as well as some identifying characteristics and details such as physical properties, occupations, and places of residence, have been changed to protect the privacy and identities of those involved.

Second Edition February 2022
Originally published by Mereo Books, December 2020

ISBN 978-1-954000-33-9 (paperback)
ISBN 978-1-954000-34-6 (eBook)

Cover design lead: Raeghan Rebstock
Editor: Nancy Laning

Published by Publish Authority
Newport Beach, CA & Roswell, GA USA
PublishAuthority.com

Printed in the United States of America

To love and peace.

Contents

PREFACE

Perhaps someday I will crawl back home, beaten, defeated. But not as long as I can make stories out of my heartbreak, beauty out of sorrow.

— SYLVIA PLATH

The year 2019 brought me so much pain, more than my body could bear. Eventually, this pain came pouring out of me and onto these pages. This is a story of love and how war changed the fate of two lovers. It is the story of a Libyan woman coming back to the homeland after graduating from England, full of dreams and ambitions, of how she fell in love with a wonderful, brave man before her world imploded in the aftermath of the "Arab Spring."

This is my story about the harrowing experiences in a country that came unraveled like a house of cards in 2011 and of how I witnessed Libya's history in the making. It is about living in a country divided by war, where the sound of rockets serenaded the people to sleep, where one's city or family name could be a 'legitimate' reason for someone to end your life. It is about the countless times I sneaked out of the house to see my boyfriend in a city whose streets were dotted with heavy machinery and militias. It is a place where something so simple and beautiful as having my Mediterranean hair blow-dried at the hairdresser ahead of a date becomes "Mission Impossible."

'Buried in My Heart' is a metaphor for all the beautiful dreams, memories, places, and people that got buried so deeply within my broken heart. I either buried things to protect and keep me going, or things got buried within me because there was no place for them to flourish and breathe anymore.

Even though my love story is told through major life-changing events in Libya's recent history, it is not in any way a political statement, nor does it invalidate or cancel anybody's reality of the same period. It just was not possible for me to tell my love story without explaining the context it happened in.

The story spans a period of many years, from 2007 until 2019, with information and facts about Libya and everything that has happened to me while attempting—often unsuccessfully—to live a normal life.

This book is a testament to resiliency and my humble attempt to honour a beautiful soul.

Please read it with compassion and an open mind.

Somewhere beyond right and wrong, there is a garden,
    I will meet you there.

— RUMI

INTRODUCTION

The book is about a love story of a Libyan couple narrated through life-changing events in Libya. The author talks about her relationship with a Libyan guy and how it was tragically impacted during the Libyan civil war, the collapse of the Qadhafi regime, and her friendship with the late US Ambassador Chris Stevens. Although the book talks about her love story; it discusses other themes such as resilience, fear of the unknown, losing control over her life, her identity and how she could not belong during the time she had spent studying in the UK, her love to her Motherland, all the things you gradually lose when you live in a war zone.

The book is a personal account as told through the author's lens about how she felt about the events that changed Libya and, ultimately, her life.

PROLOGUE

This is a love story in Libya told through the lens of its heroine. It is a first-person account of a wartime love story of a Libyan woman sharing her story, which started at the Arab Spring. Sadly, it never bloomed. Nor did the country.

It is a cautionary tale for everyone, especially the young generation in Libya.

ONE

NOT WHITE AND OUT OF PLACE: MY FORMATIVE YEARS ABROAD

I come from an illustrious family. My surname has always burdened me; it has given everybody permission to invade my life with uncomfortable questions. What is your dad like at home? How many rooms are there in your house? How many siblings do you have? Where do you live? Endless questions about my family and, for the life of me, I still do not understand the curiosity. Having a famous dad might have been a dream to many, but to me, it was not. I have always felt uneasy about it. I have tried hard to reconcile my father's public persona with the one I know, my Papa.

Many Libyan students have written their graduation thesis on his work. As such, I have had a slightly different life from many of my compatriots.

I come from Tripoli, the capital of Libya. Let me tell you about Libya: it is vast, 1.8 million square kilometres, with a low population density—not more than 6 million people. It was colonized by Italy and the Ottoman Empire prior to that. You can see the Italian influence in almost every corner of Tripoli—amazing architecture that has stood the test of time. That influence was so strong that it crawled into our kitchens as well. The Libyan cuisine is one of the best in the region: a mixture of Mediterranean, Berber, and Jewish food. It is delicious, but I would not describe it as sophisticated.

Common traits of Libyans are hospitality, incredible generosity, and stubbornness. Italians are their favourite people: they feel closer to them than others, maybe because of the historical ties, *calcio* (football), or the Mediterranean temper they both have in common. I'm not sure if the sentiment is reciprocal or even acknowledged, but that is how they feel.

I grew up in Europe in the 80s with a mother who was a beautician and my very famous father. Unlike my older sister, who embraced my father's fame and basked in its glory, I retreated into the shadows. I removed my surname on admission papers and doctors' clinics to remain anonymous and avoid the astonished looks and the happy faces when they discovered whose daughter I was. My family had moved a lot between Eastern Europe and England before finally moving back to Libya while I remained in England to pursue a quality education. The separation from my family was painful, but my father told me that my education was the surest way to a bright future—well, he was right, but little did he know what that future had in store for me some 20 years later.

Although Libya was in the centre of the atlas I had known at home and school in Libya, I struggled to locate it on any other maps. Libya was not in the centre of anything; in fact, most people did not know where it was. Just when I thought I had escaped the weight of my surname, other troubles surfaced, and coming from Libya became a problem. I often found myself defending my origins. My peers in England had little interest in me once they realised I had come from a place they had no idea existed. However, to the older generations, Libya meant trouble:

the Lockerbie bombing, the sanctions, Qadhafi, and the IRA. Such was the legacy of Libya in the 1980s and 1990s, and being a Libyan meant my fellow Libyans and I were on the wrong side of geography.

I was never really bullied; however, I was an outsider. It was always funny how I would experiment with different names at Starbucks. I would give the barista an easily recognized name to avoid the awkwardness of having to enunciate my name.

I did not belong. I was not accepted. I was not 'figured out.' I was always the coloured student. I thought I was white just because my skin was not black, but then I realised people had a whole spectrum of colours. I could not locate my race on any application forms. I was not African, even though my country is in the north of Africa. This narrative did not exist when I was a child growing up. I was not aware of who I was or what I represented to the world.

Being an outsider permitted people to invade me. Do you live in the desert? Do the women drive? Is Qadhafi dangerous? Is he crazy? Do you have to cover your hair when you go out? How come you speak English? Are you happy to be out of Libya? Are you Muslim or a practising Muslim? I had no idea that you had to be one or the other. Are you Sunni or Shia? Again, I found myself with labels and identities pinned on me by external factors (my father, geography, origin, religion, etc.)

———

How do I love thee? Let me count the ways

— ELIZABETH BROWNING

'England will always have a special place in my heart. I love her! I love the cobblestone streets, the monuments, Earl Grey tea, the books of Hanif Kureishi, and the spectacular green scenery in the north. I love how the English take care of their gardens; they are their pride and joy. Their gnomes greeted me every morning on my way to school. I love the public libraries, where I could easily spend an entire day. Greggs is another place I love, with the delicious smell of cheese and onions that always fills the shop.

I spent many years in the northeast of England – namely, Newcastle upon Tyne. But I have to say, Durham is the jewel of the north: absolutely stunning! I adored the Geordie accent and how the shop assistants called me 'pet,' a Geordie term of endearment. No matter how cold it got out there, it never stopped the beautiful Geordie lasses from partying in style in high heels and flattering dresses. The streets of Newcastle, on the weekends, always smelled of possibilities and love. I would be on my way home around 17:00 or 18:00 and see groups of ladies, of guys together, others heading to a hen party, all dressed to the nines, ready for the night. I was like a child looking at toys beautifully displayed in a shop store window at Christmas, intrigued by what was inside.

The radio became my companion. I loved BBC Radio 4 and its series 'The Archers.' BBC Radio One was also pleasant. I discovered the amazing British sense of humour through the various radio programmes. It was my way to get into their society, to listen to their stories.

Growing up in an artistic family helped me cultivate a refined taste for the art and culture scene in England. My time there was filled with glamorous evenings at the opera, weekends at galleries, piano recitals, and plays at theatres. I am also an avid reader, and because I found it challenging to have many friends there, books and Waterstone's—the major bookshop chain—were my constant companions.

However, many years later, I was able to make some wonderful friends, mostly from Mediterranean countries. We had a lot in common. They accepted me.

To be honest, I did not know quite how I felt about Libya. I believe I had always loved her in some subtle way. One thing I knew for sure was that she cast a long shadow. She was a pariah state. Loving her and understanding her were things I had constantly postponed.

Two

The Golden Era: Libya's Best and Final Years, 2003–2010

I dreaded the moment of going back to Libya in 2007. I was afraid to face the real world. I was scared to cut the umbilical cord with England and be disconnected from my friends, from a world of theatre, paintings, musicals, and the Lake District. However, I could not have come back at a better time: Libya had succeeded in ending its isolation and had transformed itself from a pariah state into a full member of the international community. Colonel Muammar Qadhafi's announcement in December 2003 that he would renounce the weapons of mass destruction programme was a significant step forward in this regard. It paved the way for the resumption and normalization of bilateral relations with the United States and lifting international sanctions. In May 2006, Libya was finally removed from the US state sponsors of terrorism list, marking its full reintegration.

———

My Little America
> She quietly expected great things to happen to her,
> and no doubt that's one of the reasons why they did.

> — ZELDA FITZGERALD (2007-2012)

Libya was flourishing. Expats were everywhere; hotel lobbies teemed with tourists. Businessmen scouted the landscape for opportunities. Everybody wanted to see the Libya of Qadhafi, the one he shielded from the rest of the world.

I started giving English courses in the evening at a private school while looking for my dream job, which, at that time, was to work in an international establishment where I could meet and work with a high calibre of people. I wanted to be in a bubble that would help my transition to Libya.

There was a newspaper in English called 'Tripoli Post,' which I liked and purchased weekly. I was excited at the thought of having printed publications in English available in Libya—everything in English had been banned there during the 1980s. The Tripoli Post often featured job openings. One day when I least expected it, I came across an opening at the US Embassy as a Protocol Assistant. I felt the job suited me and applied immediately. In my heart of hearts, I was so confident that I would get that job. A few days later, I received a phone call inviting me to go to the embassy for a written test which went well. A few days after that, I was called back for an interview, and again I felt I had done well. The next day, they called me to ask for the required papers and documents to start. I got the job!

I was happy beyond words. I belonged! I had found a separate world that existed without my knowledge, like the secret garden of an abandoned house. That was how the embassy in Libya felt to me. It was my long-sought haven. I was extremely lucky and felt humbled to have been given this opportunity to be part of this enclave.

The American diplomats were friendly, down-to-earth, and worldly, and they spoke Arabic. I was in awe of them. They were different from the insular crowd I was used to in Europe, and I felt right at home. They instantly warmed to me and started inviting me to their homes on weekends for a movie night or a cook-off. An old lady at the embassy, Ms. Cecile, was like an aunty to me. She was protective of me and always talked to me about love and men and how I would be better off with a foreigner and not a Libyan.

I remember one time I was at the photocopier in the corridor when she walked past me, stopped for a second, then made her way back to me. I had on a white blouse. She looked at me and whispered very quietly: "Sara, sweetheart, next time you wear a white blouse, make sure you wear a white bra with it'. I was mortified. I said: "but I have a white vest underneath my blouse, can you still see my bra?"She replied: "It is pink," and walked off. Nowadays, every time I wear a white blouse with a white bra, I remember that incident fondly.

Ms. Cecile often entertained at the weekends, inviting diplomats from other embassies. She always made sure I was invited. She would ask me to show up earlier than the other guests so we could have some time to ourselves to chat and exchange some gossip. My network soon widened, and I felt sequestered, but in a nice way. My Libyan colleagues were equally charming. Many, like myself, were either born or brought up abroad. Needless to say, they did not waste any time passing on the information about my father to the American colleagues. They wanted to meet him.

Part of my function was to organise and attend receptions. The crème de la crème of Libyan society was there, from all walks of life—doctors, businessmen, authors, designers, all of whom had studied in the US back in the 60s and 70s—and were quite nostalgic for the US. The Americans knew how to cultivate contacts and threw upscale events. The only nuisance about those gatherings was the Internal Intelligence guys of the regime, who used to park outside the diplomats' houses to keep track of who mingled with the Americans. Even though Americans were welcome in Libya, they were under scrutiny, along with everyone who came in contact with them. No amount of bilateral agreements, receptions, or Fourth of July parties would remove the stains of the bad blood between the two countries.

Libya was a Family Duty Station, which meant that the diplomats had their families there. Their children went to the American School. They lived in houses, like us, across the city. There were no security guards at their homes, and they did not live in a compound. They moved freely around Tripoli.

Summer was the best time for gathering. They all welcomed me into their homes and families. I, of course, obliged. I still remember the nice mini-burgers they prepared, the smell of grass, the laughter of the children, how the couples displayed their affection to one another from time to time. It was endearing. I would ask them how they had met, and they would tell me all kinds of stories. Some had been together since High School. They shared stories from their first dates, how they had proposed. They were unbelievably warm people. I cannot say enough how much they meant to me. I could not wait for my life to start—to find my 'happily ever after,' to have a place to call my own and to have movie nights and entertain guests with my partner.

One of the most amazing colleagues I knew and worked closely with was the late Chris Stevens. When the embassy reopened, they started working out of a hotel and had four floors dedicated to them. One day, I was on my way to the floor above me to chat with Ms. Cecile when I started fiddling with my earrings, and one of them fell off. The corridor had a red carpet with yellow patterns, and I could not locate the missing earring, and I got down on my knees trying to find it. I was outside a closed door when it suddenly opened, and I saw black shoes in front of me. I looked up and saw this dashing man. He smiled confidently and said, 'What are you doing?' That was how I met Chris Stevens.

In 2007 he was the Deputy Chief of Mission (the DCM). He and I became close friends, exchanging stories about our lives, families, near-miss romances. We shared a love of literature. I introduced him to the writings of E.E. Cummings and Anne Sexton, and he introduced me to the work of Roya Hakakian. He was like George Clooney and Clint Eastwood wrapped into one. He was my closest and best friend, and he became a big part of my life. I adored him.

Chris was an avid tennis player and a man with a tremendous range of interests. It was always enriching talking to him. Despite his busy schedule, he always read the books, articles, and poems I shared with him and always found the time to discuss them with me.

On my 28th birthday, he threw a surprise birthday gathering for me at the embassy. His cook made a lovely birthday cake for me; it was simple and beautiful. Chris, Ms. Cecile, and I often did things together. We went to the beach, to birthdays and brunches. Ms. Cecile always teased him about the ladies who tried to approach him and chat him up at parties.

I remember the first time I visited his house. It was beautifully decorated with memories of places in which he had served. It had furniture from Syria, Morocco, and Egypt, seating cushions and decorated doors from Syria, antique rugs from Egypt, and paintings from Jerusalem. The house was spotless, and the cook carefully prepared weekly meals neatly wrapped up in the fridge.

I had the great honour of meeting his father, stepmother, and stepsister, who came to visit him in 2008. They had a nice tour of the country. Ms. Cecile invited us all to her house for dinner to honour them.

I was living my happiest days. The world was my oyster. As Virginia Woolf so eloquently put it, 'I am rooted, but I flow.' As long as I was able to use 'summer' as a verb and travel to quench my thirst for knowledge, I had no problems living in Libya. I was content. Libya was not perfect, but it was on the right track. It was alive, blossoming, and thriving, and the country was safe. Some would argue that it was safe for all the wrong reasons, but that was not something I was concerned about. I was safe, and that was enough. Maybe you will think this was selfish, or rather a narrow view of life on my part, but keep reading until the end, and you will understand.

Libyans never had to think about electricity, petrol or water. Household utilities were free, as they were subsidised. We owned our houses. Our cash was always available in the banks. These were things we took for granted. You could go out at any time of the day, and nobody would bother you. You could leave your car unlocked while you did your shopping, and nobody would touch it.

Businesses, new cafés, and restaurants were mushrooming all

over Tripoli. A Schengen visa (for limited visits) was made accessible to Libyans within ten working days. My dilemma—and the dilemma of others as well —in those days was limited to my weekends and holiday destinations: London, Malta, or Prague? People were relaxed. You could sense it, smell it in the air. Unfortunately, that would soon change, but little did we know. We were high on the 'New Libya,' the 'Libya of Tomorrow.'

THREE

THE MAN WITH CHESTNUT HAIR

If two people love each other, there can be no happy ending
to it

— ERNEST HEMINGWAY

2010

I do not remember the exact moment I laid eyes on him—I
was either driving back from work or driving around one
summer evening—but I do remember how I felt. Something caught my eye and tugged at my heartstrings. He was tall,
slim, and dark, and I wanted to know him.

I decided to drive back to get a closer look. There was something rugged and untamed about this man. His chestnut hair was
free and wild, like an Arabian horse. His charisma filled the air; it
was almost overpowering. Guys were all over him like flies on
honey. I knew he was different. It was a moment that set a chain
of events in motion, changing my life irrevocably.

I made a habit of driving past the corner where I had first

noticed him, and I saw him almost every time I did so. He was a magnet. The way he looked and dressed, I knew he did not conform. It did not take him long to notice me, and a coy dance started between us. There was a haunting quality to him that I could not quite put my finger on. I was drawn to him but scared.

You need to understand that meeting opportunities for young men and women dwindle after university in a semi-conservative society like Libya. So, if a girl and a guy sparked in a café or if they happen to be driving alongside each other—hands on the wheel, I know—it was customary for the guy to try and talk to the girl, give her his number so that contact could be established.

I would go to the embassy very excited at the thought of driving home past his usual spot and seeing him. He often had a number of guys around him. I wanted to figure him out. Sometimes he would be talking to guys his own age; other times, he would be talking to men who were old enough to be his grandfather. *Who is this guy that everybody seemed to like? I thought.*

The Encounter

When I first met her, I knew in a moment
　I would have to spend the next few days re-arranging my mind
　So there would be room for her to stay.

— SCOTT FITZGERALD

After years of hard work, I got promoted and became the head of the protocol section. I was a supervisor, with staff! Among my many tasks, I was involved in preparing high-level visits from 'Congressional Delegations' or CODELs, senior members of the State Department. During my time with the embassy, I had met the then Secretary of State Condoleezza Rice, the then Permanent Chair of the 2008 Democratic National Convention, Nancy Pelosi, and the late Senator John McCain. Towards the end of my time with the embassy, I met Secretary of State Hillary Clinton and worked with her special team before her visit, which took place in 2011.

One very hot summer afternoon in June, in the middle of the preparations for the Fourth of July reception, I drove home, and again I passed the chestnut-haired guy's place. I did not see him, but then a car drove in the opposite direction past me, and there he was. He leaned out of the window and asked me to stop. I went slowly, unsure whether I should stop or keep driving. He turned the car around and followed me. I kept moving, then stopped. He came to my car, said hello, and asked how I was doing. He introduced himself: his name was Mohamed. He then asked if we could exchange numbers. We did, although I stumbled on my very own phone number. I was not good at Arabic numbers; they come out in reverse. He suppressed a smile at my attempt to get the number correctly and suggested giving me his number instead. I said no. He took my number and gave me a missed call to save it.

I drove home happy and nervous in equal measures. *There is no going back now,* I thought.

I reached home. It was Thursday night—the weekend was here. My imagination ran wild that night, worrying about him calling my number in the middle of the night, drunk, slurring inappropriate words. I got so scared I turned my mobile to silent, and I fell asleep.

I woke up Friday morning, and the first thing I did was reach out for my mobile. I illuminated the screen, and I looked: NO MISSED CALLS. What? Why? How come? I was relieved but also disappointed.

Days went by, and that phone call never arrived. I saw him a few times on the streets. He just smiled politely and waved at me —no phone calls, though. One evening, I mustered all the courage I had and dialed his number, not sure if he would know who it was. He answered. He was calm, collected, and very polite. He detected my not-so-fluent Arabic right away and asked if I had been living abroad. I said yes. He then asked how old I was. Thirty, I said. You look much younger, he replied. I asked him why he had not reached out, and he simply said, 'I did not want to bother you, and sometimes I would be with the guys. They often use profanities, and I did not want to expose you to that. You were always welcome to call me, though,' he concluded.

I was gravely disappointed. I wanted an enthusiastic man who could not wait to talk to me. He was rather too composed and controlled. Yet I was in awe of him, despite my grave disappointment.

————

OUR FIRST DATE

I saw the dreamer in her had fallen in love with me and she did not know it.

That moment the dreamer in me fell in love with her and I knew it.

— TED HUGHES

One day while I was at the office, I decided to call this man with the chestnut hair to tell him I would stop by to see him on my way home. I was counting the minutes until I arrived. I called him, and he came to see me. He asked me to park my car properly on the sidewalk (we park any way we like in Libya) and ride with him. I did, but I was nervous. I put my bag on my left side between us just to stop any attempts from him to touch me if that thought ever crossed his mind.

We drove off to the beach, which was a few minutes from where I had parked my car. I felt safe. He did not speak much at first. He was silently watching the sun and the waves. He pointed at the sea and said, 'I love the sea very much.' Then he started talking about his life and the dating scene in Libya. He explained how girls often tried to manipulate men into marrying them, which made him very guarded. His relationships were casual, fleeting sexual encounters, and he did not like to fall in love. It made him feel weak and helpless.

He was not the typical invasive Libyan with all their uncomfortable questions. He did not ask about my family, so of course, I did not volunteer that information. I felt at ease with him. He did not try to impress me. He was himself, not an ounce of disingenuousness about him.

I learned that day that he was six years my senior, had graduated from the Business Management School, and did not have a steady job; he'd done a little bit of this, a little bit of that, breeding dogs, renting houses to people. He was so at peace with who he was. You see, when Libyans find out that someone had spent the majority of their life abroad, they will try their hardest to get to know them, to impress them, to befriend them, to show them that they knew this pop singer or that rock band. I got none of that from him. He did not try to impress me. I was a pristine princess who could hardly speak Arabic and always had a structured path to live, sleeping at 22:00, waking up at 06:00—he was the complete opposite. I was smitten.

One of the most personal things about me is my long-lasting love for the English language. I felt alive in it. However, somehow, the fact that he did not speak a word of English seemed irrelevant. I felt whole with him. Life would never be the same. I knew he would reside in my heart and mark me for many years to come.

There was tenderness in his eyes but also such intensity that I could hardly look directly at them. He was well-mannered, which was not how he came across at first. How he looked and how he carried himself were at odds with each other, and I was shocked to my core. I expected a vulgar guy, but instead, I found someone with kind eyes, a nice smile, very considerate. He touched my soul.

When the date ended, he drove me back to my car, and he said to me that he would be there for me if I needed a friend to chat with, but it would be unwise if we were to embark on a relationship now. Needless to say, my heart sank; I felt thwarted. I went back home, knowing I had fallen harder than I cared to control.

I appreciated his honesty, but not because I understood it. I appreciated it because it was the only thing I could have done at the time. It was years later that I understood how wise he had been. You do not commit to a relationship from the very first date, however many butterflies there are in your stomach.

———

They slipped briskly into an intimacy from which they never
recovered.

— SCOTT FITZGERALD

Mohamed and I took things slowly. No relationship, no claims
over each other, but we kept seeing each other and talking from
time to time. Despite the incredible chemistry and attraction, he
respected my physical and emotional space, and I reciprocated.
At the end of the summer of 2010, we were moving towards a
relationship. We became romantic, and our meetings took on the
shape of dates. I loved him, so much so that I visibly shivered
whenever I saw him, sometimes to the point where driving was
not possible anymore. I had to pull over until my legs relaxed—I
was driving a stick shift, you see.

Mohamed filled my whole life, and I filled his. His eyes were
happy, dancing, smiling every time he saw me. His kisses were
beautiful, soft. He had beautiful hands—dark, strong, long
fingers. I loved holding his hands, interlocking our fingers. I
loved them. I would hide my head deep in his chest, and I was
home: he was home. He was Libya, my Libya.

We used to go to the beach together. I would drive to the
usual spot in the early morning, leave my car and ride with him.
We would buy some refreshments and fruit on the way. I am not
much of a swimmer, but Mohamed was an excellent one. He
would take a boat, and we would go far into the sea. I would stay
on the boat, and he would dive and disappear. Then I would beg
him to take me back to the shore. I would step off the boat, the
heat of the sands hurting the soles of my feet, then run to our
room and take a nap there. We were not the only couple there—
love was in the air!

Before any trip to the beach together, I had to make several shopping trips to various places to get 'bikini ready.' Going to the beach was a process that had to commence days before; I could not just agree to go on the spot. I had to find the right bikini and, most importantly, the right Cache Maiollt, and do not even get me started on the waxing. I am not a guy, after all. Guys have it easy. They put on some shorts, and bam, you are good to go! But for us—it's a different story. I wish guys would understand!

One night during the summer of 2010, I went out to see Mohamed. He took me in his car, and we drove off to a faraway place. It was on the outskirt of Tripoli, his friend's farm. We entered the small house on the farm, which was stuffy and hot. There were geckos on the walls. We lay next to each other on one of the mattresses on the floor. He caressed my back, kissed my forehead, and played with my hair. He was so nice to me and treated me gently, sincerely, and protectively. That night is still vividly emblazoned on my mind, 11 years later.

FOUR

THE JASMINE REVOLUTION

2010-2011

It was December 2010, cold, wet and beautiful. Chris Stevens' assignment as DCM came to an end in the summer of 2009. It had been difficult saying goodbye to him. Everybody at the embassy was crying that day. He moved back to DC to study for another master's at the National War College, but the events that unfolded in the coming months in Libya would play a pivotal role in sending him back to us, forever changing his life. Chris and I remained in touch, and I saw him in the States on subsequent visits.

The holiday season was upon us, but I did not want to spend the New Year abroad. I wanted to be in Libya with Mohamed. He was all I ever wanted. I did, however, travel for a week to Brussels before the New Year to see my best friend—a Greek girl, Maria, whom I met while studying in the UK. She met this handsome Belgian guy, Jacob, on one of those marvelous Greek beaches, and by the end of the summer, they were a couple.

Maria went back with him to Belgium to start a new chapter in her life, and I went to Brussels to visit her. She was living with Jacob in a flat in Brussels, which was small and modern but cozy. The warmth of her flat engulfed me. It was like a pair of caring arms around me. To be living here, tucked away in such a beautiful place, with a hot chocolate while watching the snowflakes dance outside your window—that was heaven to me! I imagined myself in her kitchen, making hot chocolate for my boyfriend and me. Why couldn't I have that? It was sad.

I loved how easy it was for her just to rent a place and live with her boyfriend. I could not do that in Libya. I considered myself lucky for having such supportive, understanding parents, but moving out of their house and shacking up with my partner was not something to contemplate. It was against the culture. Instead, I had to meet Mohamed in my car or his. Couples do meet in cafés in Libya, it is not frowned upon, but if you wanted some intimacy, you would need to think of creative ways of finding it, hence the car.

Maria and I made cupcakes together, and she invited some friends over for some crudités to meet me. We had a lovely time together, huddled around her Christmas tree. I loved Brussels. It was festive, and the smell of Belgian waffles wafted through the crisp air. I bought some gifts for Mohamed: cologne, a belt, body lotion, and some chocolate.

Mohamed and I met as soon as I got back, needless to say, in his car. I could not hold enough of him in my hands. I wanted to be a part of him, to attach myself to him. I tried to look at him, kiss him, hold him, and talk to him—all at once—to make sure we truly existed at that moment. I always felt like there was not enough time for all of that. He would often laugh at me, pull me to his chest and kiss my forehead. He knew what I was trying to do.

One day while I was going about my daily tasks at work without a care in the world, I overheard my Libyan colleagues talking with concerned faces about something that sounded ominous from what I could gather. I did not care about it at first. I did not have that radar that makes you detect trouble before it starts, though later, I became an expert.

After days of these chats under their breath, I decided to ask one of my colleagues, and he told me that there was a revolution happening in Tunisia. I worked so hard to suppress my laughter. I had no reference for that. People did not go out and protest in this region.

Although Tunisia had been ruled by one party since 1987, it was considered one of the most liberal, tolerant countries in the region. The strong influence of the French had never really ceased. Besides, their President had the support of Qadhafi, and who could defy Qadhafi? But I was sorely mistaken.

There was a young Tunisian guy whose name would soon signify the start of this era, Mohamed Bouazizi, a street vendor who sold vegetables. He was asked by a female officer one day to remove his cart because he was illegally stationed; he refused. She confiscated the cart, and after a heated argument, she slapped him. Feeling humiliated, he set himself on fire. That instigated public outrage in Tunisia, which gathered momentum and spread across the country. The protesters filled the streets, vandalizing cars and shops and demanding economic and security reforms.

Coming back home from work during those days, I would often find my parents in their living room with coffee and sweets, watching the news coverage on Tunisia and debating the current debacle. I would dash quickly to the kitchen, hoping to find that a nice hearty lunch had been kept for me. Walking into the kitchen, I often found that the winter evening sun had made its way in before me, painting the kitchen walls and the floor with its glorious warm orange rays. I would settle for whatever meal was prepared, grab an orange and some fennel and go off to my bedroom. I was acutely aware of the background noises, and they made me very uncomfortable: the angry voices of the protesters, the journalists commentating on the unfolding events. I kept my door closed. I did not want the noises to seep through the walls of my bedroom. I would spend the evenings in my bedroom, reading a book, deciding what to wear the next day to work, calling my boyfriend.

The Tunisian President desperately tried all measures to restore order, trying to appease the public by creating new jobs and reshuffling his cabinet, but it was too late. The fear barrier had been broken, and there was no going back.

I celebrated New Year's Eve at home with my parents. A few minutes before midnight, I called Mohamed. I wanted to welcome 2011 with him. He whispered to me, 'I love you.' It was midnight, January 1, 2011.

On January 14, the Tunisian President fled the country under Libyan protection. Something worrying was going on. My colleagues were right. I started to pay attention.

THE 25 JANUARY REVOLUTION – EGYPT

On January 25, riots erupted in Egypt. Protesters came pouring out onto the streets and public plazas, demanding an end to the Mubarak regime ruling Egypt since 1981. The protesters swept the country and rejected all the televised pleas made by the President to the public promising reforms and new elections. On 11 February 2011, the resignation of the Egyptian President was announced, handing power over to the Supreme Council of the

Armed Forces. Bewildered Libyans were left, literally, in the middle, stunned.

For the uninitiated, Libya is located between Tunisia and Egypt. Being rich in oil, our pride, and joy, Libya depended on foreign labourers from those neighbouring countries and beyond. Much to my embarrassment, many Libyans maintained a superior view of themselves to those of other countries.

I started following the domino effect, thinking somehow we would be spared, that this wave would not engulf us. This was Libya, after all.

The events in Tunisia and Egypt had cloaked all everyday discussions. My parents were to be found at their usual place in their living room, with their evening rituals of coffee and Libyan delights, some biscuits from the local shop. My sister stayed in her room following the events on her television. She would occasionally storm out of her room, following important breaking news, running downstairs and shouting: 'Papa, Mama, did you see what happened?' They would exchange some thoughts, express their astonishment, and then she would go back to her room until the next big announcement. If she passed me in the hallway, she would repeat what she had seen. I could not muster any excitement or share in her enthusiasm. I was inundated and unmoored. I thought if only I had Harry Potter's magic wand, I would hide Libya on the map for a few weeks until this storm had blown over.

My Libyan colleagues were taking turns playing political analyst of the month. It was unusual and unprecedented— Libyans never discussed politics, nor was it a part of their discourse and existence. Qadhafi was never mentioned in public. People could not say his name without looking over their shoulders. To me, he was an integral part of Libya; he was there long before I existed. He was like the Red Castle, which is an ancient castle right in the heart of the capital. I never feared him or felt his infamous 'Iron Fist.' One thing for sure is that he was not as demonized in Libya as the outside media outlets would have you believe. But then again, as I said at the beginning of the book, my reality does not cancel anybody else's who lived in Libya at any given time.

FIVE

LIBYA'S WINTER, MY FOREVER AUTUMN

It takes courage to die for a cause, but also to live for one.

— AZAR NAFISI

I had never had any presence on social media platforms. I was very private due to my father's visibility, I guess, or maybe this was just who I really was. Facebook was pretty much happening in Libya. My colleagues and friends were talking about a possible demonstration planned to take place in the East of Libya, namely the city of Benghazi. Benghazi is the second-largest city in Libya and is 652km from the capital. The date the activists chose was February 15. Everybody was scared, monitoring the Facebook pages. I was not convinced. I thought Qadhafi would crush any attempt at compromising the stability of the country.

One of my team asked for leave during the week of 13–17 February to stay home with his family, out of harm's way. I agreed and said I would cover for him. He looked at me and said: 'Sara, this is serious!' I still remember how red his face was, how he was measuring his words carefully. He said, 'The regime will be overthrown.'

Libya has a different social fabric from that of Egypt or Tunis. Libyan society is a tribal society, by and large. Loyalties and allegiances lie with the tribe, not the country. The armed forces and battalions were primarily composed of tribes that had strong historical ties with the Qadhafi tribe. If anything were to destabilize that fabric, it would rip the country to pieces and ensue unprecedented chaos. It was complicated.

True to their promise, the protesters took to the streets of Benghazi, demanding the removal of Qadhafi. My Libyan colleagues were so tense, going up and down the stairs of the embassy talking to each other, checking videos of the protests online. My family was scared, to say the least. The Libyan television broadcasts continued as usual. On the other hand, the international TV channels were covering the story every hour on the hour.

While the East was rocking the cradle, the capital was eerie. You could sense people's panic in the air. In a pre-emptive move to deter any possible thought of going out in solidarity with the east, loyalists took to the streets, driving cars draped with the Libyan flag and posters of Qadhafi while playing celebratory songs of the Brother Leader - Qadhafi. The air was dense with them, like a humid August day. They were roaming the streets, parking in front of petrol stations, and around the main Green Square in the heart of the capital. They were not intimidating anybody, but they made sure people registered their presence. We are here! I was fine with that. I was never a political person, nor did I wish to be. I knew no harm would come my way. I was a simple, ordinary citizen trying to live my life.

Meanwhile, my relationship continued developing, getting stronger and sweeter. I had Mohamed saved on my mobile as

'Sweetheart,' but whenever we had a silly 'lovers' squabble,' I would change 'Sweetheart' to 'Hemar,' which means donkey in Arabic. 'Donkey' is used as an insult in the wider Arab culture, but funnily enough, it can also be used as a term of endearment. I could not have thought about him more, even if I had wanted to. Mohamed was like wallpaper, the background photo on a laptop: always there. He pervaded everything.

The embassy was quiet. The Americans were silent; the way they looked was disconcerting. I started to feel uneasy. But I thought the riots would be stopped and nipped in the bud. This country had been spared for 42 years. I did not even know what gunfire sounded like; fireworks scared me. But you never really know what life can throw at you and the many subtle ways through which it could challenge, change and test you. I would not have imagined that I would be driving next to anti-missiles, tanks, and heavy weaponry one day, and not a single hair would fall out of place. War changes people; It reveals them. It shows them sides to themselves they did not know they had. War kills innocence.

There are moments in everybody's life when something happens, and after that, everything you experience will be marked by those moments. Your life will be tarnished forever by them. They will be used when describing or recalling events, memories: the before and after. This is what 2011 is to me and many others. There was my life before 2011 and my life afterward.

Tripoli has always been a lively city; shops stay open till after midnight. Expats living comfortably. The cafés are the best in Libya: clean, modern, and spacious. Hands on heart, the best place for a cup of coffee or cappuccino is Libya. You have to know this about Libyans: they take their coffee very seriously.

There was one café in particular that many Libyans and

expats love, called O2. It is right next to the beach and has the best pancakes; many Americans can attest to that. I used to go on Friday mornings with a couple of Libyan colleagues and a few Americans. We would have some coffee, cappuccino, and pancakes with either chocolate or maple syrup. All of that changed overnight. The shops started closing early, and people rushed to the stores, stocking up on food. One day, when I was driving back from work, I saw a man standing next to his blue car with the boot open. The boot was full of oil, milk crates, and flour packets. His wife was coming out of the store with bags in both hands. A collective panic was sweeping the streets. People were literally running in and out of the stores buying bags of groceries. It was cold and gloomy. This scene is still etched on my mind. I went home feeling bad. The weighty realisation that I had tried so hard to deny started to dawn on me, and Harry Potter's magic wand was not going to help me.

On the night of the 16th, other cities defected and joined the East in protesting. They were now asking Qadhafi to leave the country. Well-known figures in high ranks defected that night also. The embassy sent us a text message asking us to remain at home the following day, the 17th. The city was dead. The tension was palpable; you could cut it with a knife. There was not a single car in sight. I used to hear the cars as they drove by my bedroom overlooking the highway. The silence was deafening; no more screeching or squealing. I realised that my bed made a squeaking sound. *Had it always made that sound*, I wondered? That's how quiet it was.

We huddled in the main living room, my sister, brother, and parents. It was cold and rainy outside. We watched the news on different channels, but the Libyan channels were apparently still in denial. They were playing songs on repeat!

On the day of the 17th, my dad's only sister, whom he adores infinitely, called him. She asked if she could come over and spend the night with us. She was so scared listening to all the rumours about what might take place that night. The text messaging services on the mobile networks were disabled, and everybody's balance was topped up automatically by the phone company as a bonus. The phone companies had the habit of sending free credits to everybody in the country ahead of a religious celebration or a national day as a gift. But what was the occasion now? Maybe that was an attempt to boost our morale. Not being able to text your friends and family, and with an ample free balance, people were left with no choice but to call each other. And do I need to say it? To talk about what was happening.

Tripoli became a ghost town. I went out very quickly to the local shop, but the shelves were empty. It was so sad. I bought comfort stuff—chocolate, biscuits, Pepsi, noodles—and grabbed random things, thinking they might become scarce, and I would regret not buying them when I had the chance. I also made a trip to the pharmacy, where I bought bars of soap, toothpaste, sanitary towels, deodorants, then went home, resisting the urge to splurge on crisps and other treats. I had to be sensible.

I hid in my room and started watching cartoons. I did not want to see how helpless my parents were. I watched Studio Ghibli's movies and was instantly taken away to their beautiful world. For a brief moment, I forgot about the news and the many, many questions that were swimming inside my foggy head.

One night, while we were watching the news, there was suddenly some breaking news broadcast by a specific news channel claiming that Qadhafi had fled Libya to Venezuela. A few seconds later, we heard some guys shouting far away. The sound echoed back to us. Apparently, the echo was not the only thing roaming the streets that night. The guys were shouting happily, 'Qadhafi ran away, he ran away!' We stood up and started to move slowly on our toes towards the main door. Even though the voices were far away, we locked the main door to our house that night for the very first time.

I checked my email the following morning and found a lot of emails from my American colleagues who had served at one point in Libya. They were all asking about my family and me and saying that I should stay safe; Chris was one of them. I was touched by their thoughts and love but scared and angry as well. I was scared because if they were concerned about me, the situation was far more serious than I wanted to acknowledge. I was angry because, deep down, I did not want to accept what was going on. Awful thoughts popped into my mind and stayed there like an annoying guest at dinner who overstays their welcome.

A few days later, the internet was blocked, and we were cut off from the outside world. Many wealthy businessmen withdrew huge amounts of money from the banks, creating a severe shortage in liquidity. I went to the bank, and there was a ceiling on withdrawal, a concept unheard of before this chaos. I withdrew 500 LYD, which is worth $100 now. Before 2011, 1 LYD was equal to between 1.15 and 1.20 USD, and we complained! Later, in 2017, it would be one dollar to 9 LYD.

Foreigners were fleeing Libya. The airport was packed, and people were so scared that they slept at the airport ahead of their flights. Everybody wanted to jump ship. The foreign labourers and workers left. As a result, the shops, cafés, bakeries, restaurants, and many businesses shut down in a matter of days. The city was paralyzed. Piles of trash filled the streets.

Qadhafi appeared on TV and delivered a speech urging the Libyans to come back to their senses and heed his advice. He explained how this was a conspiracy against the country to take over our oil and resources. He was crying over spilled milk: It was far too late.

On 27 February, a National Transitional Council was formed to act as 'the political face of the revolution.' It was composed of dissidents and figures that had defected from the regime. The council quickly picked up momentum and received wide international support and recognition as the sole legitimate governing body of Libya.

After those accelerating events, a group of guys went out in the middle of the night to show their solidarity with the east and the other cities. One of them was Mohamed's youngest brother. The streets were patrolled, of course, by goons to prevent anything from happening. Unfortunately, they were seen and shot at—Mohamed's brother was hit and severely wounded. He was taken to a military hospital to be kept under surveillance to be questioned later. The news saddened me; Mohamed's voice shook when he told me. His brother was largely unconscious, and his family did not have access to him. His father was trying hard to find any connections to help him see his son. He would stay in the hospital from February until May, when he finally died, succumbing to his injuries.

Without access to the outside world, I did not know what information to believe. I could not assess the situation accurately. Libyans were killing each other. It was heartbreaking.

I could not see Mohamed as much as we would have wanted. I wanted to be there for him when his brother died, but it was not possible. Everything was closed. I had no excuse to go out, but I did sneak out of the house to see him whenever I could. Turning the car engine on was something I had to plan. Because it was so quiet outside, you could hear the tiniest of noises, and If my parents heard my car starting, they would stop me from going out. The window of their bedroom opened onto my garage. I needed to survey the house and see where everybody was, and I also needed to be in my pyjamas not to arouse their suspicions. If they were in the living room, I would make a run for it and go out to see Mohamed. He was only a few minutes away from me, so it was easy to see him. I would park in an alley, and we would sit in the car, keeping the cold at bay, sometimes in silence. It was romantic and the only sure thing in a world of uncertainties.

Coming back home was just as hard. I had to park outside the house, then enter the house, holding the key chains tightly in my hand so they would not make a sound, check where everybody was, then open the garage quietly and drive the car back in. It was exhausting, but it was worth it.

———

.

A thirty-year-old cargo boat
    stubbornly hanging on to my name and address.
    They have swabbed me clear of my loving associations.

— Sylvia Plath

Those of my American colleagues still in Tripoli called me every day to check on me, advising me to stock up on food supplies and buy the necessary items and medicine. I wanted to ask why because surely this would end in a few days, weeks at the most, but I could not; the phones were tapped. I was grateful to receive their calls. They were a much-needed lifeline. But I was scared every time I received those calls. What if someone came knocking on my door, accusing me of working with the enemy?

The DCM, Ms. Joan Polaschik, my supervisor, was the acting Chargé d'Affaires during these incredible times. She was and still is an amazing woman, a true leader, for whom I had immense respect. She called me one day and said to me, in a very emotional voice, that she and the rest of my Libyan colleagues would be leaving, but they would come back as soon as the situation allowed it, and I should stay home and be careful. That's when I knew that this was far from over. In fact, it had not even begun.

With the Americans gone, I felt homeless. I felt like a veteran who had been stripped of his medals. I had no place to belong. My suits and office clothes hung in the closet, collecting dust like the marionettes of a retired puppeteer. I now wore nothing but pyjamas. No makeup, no perfume, my hair was up in a bun. I did not like this version of me; I was not special anymore. Many more things would be chipped away later; this was just the beginning. I had nothing to wake up for anymore—just news and more depressing news. The TV was on all the time, and we were all glued in front of the screen skipping from one channel to another, trying to make sense of it all.

Suddenly I could relate to Anne Frank. This was how she must have felt, hiding in the attic. There was nothing for me to do, just long, endless stretches of nothing. I could not live without a structure, so I had to invent a new one. I started by waking up early, eating healthily, brushing up on my French, and reading books. In the afternoon, I watched 'Friends' and 'Sex and the City' again. I had never spent this much time at home before; the embassy was my home. I was lost. There was so much pent-up energy, and I had nowhere to release it. Of course, I fought a few times with my elder sister, who had always been convinced that I was jealous of her, and now she finally found all the time in the world to provoke me and get on my nerves.

One sad, empty evening, I got a craving for egg-fried rice, and I remembered all those times I had gone to the Chinese restaurant with my cousins or colleagues from the embassy. My mouth watered at the thought of those spring rolls dipped in sweet and sour sauce. With no internet to check the recipe, I tried my very best and cooked some rice, then added some eggs and stirred them together. I was so hungry I just ate it regardless of how unpalatable it was.

I spent most evenings with my family for our daily reality dose, and then I would go to bed with a heavy heart. My relationship was put on hold. My whole life came to a grinding halt.

Six

Operation Odyssey Dawn

In what language does rain fall over tormented cities?

— Pablo Neruda

March 2011

The fighting was between those who were with the regime and those against it. There was no telling who had the upper hand. An arms embargo was enforced, and NATO began its military invasion on March 19, 2011, implementing the UNSC 1973. 'Operation Odyssey Dawn' was the American code name for its role in enforcing the 1973 Resolution. There was a no-fly zone all over Libya. It was a Saturday, I still remember. I do not need a calendar to remind me of those dates.

I had a shower and sat there waiting to hear the first bomb. Would I recognize it? What sounds did bombs and shells make? And then I remembered the line quoted above, from the amazing poet Pablo Neruda: 'In what language does rain fall over tormented cities?' Rain for me here represented the bombs, of course. That is the beauty and power of poetry: it is subjective.

I was fighting back my tears. I wanted to go out and see Mohamed, but I was afraid. Air strikes started in the evening and punctuated our nights. The NATO operations would last until 21 October 2011. The house shook on occasion. I would sometimes hear the neighbours opening up their doors, conferring, trying to determine where a bomb had landed, comparing notes with each other. My brother would go up on the roof to check if he could see anything.

I was heartbroken. I felt so sorry for Libya; she was being violated and wrecked. *Could she feel this pain*, I wondered? The unrest worsened in ever-multiplying ways. As the east slipped away from Qadhafi's grip, we were still in his stronghold. International sanctions had begun to block many supply routes, and many shortages were visible. Fuel shortages were one of them; suddenly, there was no fuel. People queued outside the petrol stations for weeks. Yes, weeks!

My brother had to sell the radio from his car, and my mother topped the money up for him to buy a bicycle. He could not afford to run the car anymore. He used the bike to get us vegetables and whatever he could find. My mother started baking bread at home. All the bakeries had to shut down because there were no foreign workers. Our cleaning lady and her husband also had to leave us to return to their country. The walls were closing in on us, on Tripoli.

Many public figures appeared on Libyan television, appealing to the cities that had defected to go back and turn over a new leaf. My father grew wary that he might be approached. He found himself in a catch 22 situation. If he went on TV, he would be in the rebels' bad books; if he did not, he would be in the regime's bad books. He switched his phone off for a few days, just to gather his thoughts and find a way out of this without putting us in harm's way. If someone came knocking on our door looking for him, we were instructed to say he was away.

————

APRIL

One day, as we watched the news, I saw Chris Stevens in Benghazi. My parents both looked at me and said: 'Isn't that your friend?'

He had been sent there to coordinate with the National Transitional Council. I prayed that day that the internal intelligence guys, who knew very well that he was my friend, would not barge in on us in the living room. I imagined all kinds of morbid scenarios.

————

A CAKE FOR THE ROYAL WEDDING

Following the preparations for the wedding of Prince William and Kate was a welcome distraction. I had something to look forward to, and I was very excited for them as I waited for the long-anticipated day. On the day of the wedding, 29 April 2011, Mum and I baked a cake to go with our morning coffee and tea. It was a plain sponge cake to celebrate the happy day. We woke my sister up to join us; otherwise, she would have thrown a fit and accused us of excluding her. We sat together and watched the whole thing, and I finally saw the wedding dress that had generated all that buzz. The ceremony was beautiful, and it warmed my heart.

MAY

I remember that the first time I saw the protests in the east, people were waving a flag and claiming it to be the actual flag of Libya. I turned to my father and asked him if that was true. Was that our flag? What about the green flag? That was the only flag of Libya I had known. My father briefly explained to me its history, but I could not accept that flag. I associated it with fear and instability. I still have pain in my stomach every time I see it.

In 1951 the whole of Libya gained full independence from Italy, a flag of red-black-green horizontal tricolour flag of the Kingdom of Libya that also featured the Islamic crescent moon and five-pointed star at the centre.

1951 - 1969

Author's note: To view colour images, read the history, and more on the flag of Libya, you can go to the Wikipedia website > en.wikipedia.org/wiki/Flag_of_Libya
or here > bit.ly/3fTgKGq

The flag chosen for this era when Qadhafi came into power in 1969 was a red-white-black horizontal tricolour.

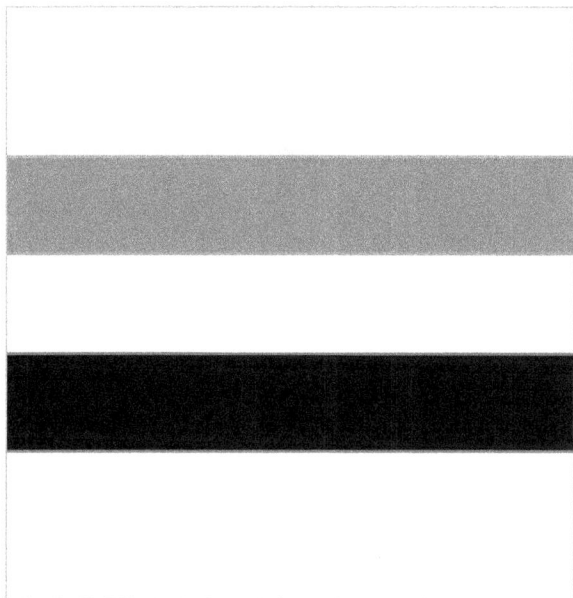

1969 - 1972

In 1972 Libya united with Egypt and Syria to create the Federation of Arab Republics. This dream was short-lived because the countries could not agree on the way forward. A coat of Arms of the Federation was added to the previous flag and located right in the centre of it.

1972 - 1977

A plain green flag was chosen in 1977 to represent Qadhafi's vision. It is arguably the only plain colour flag in the world.

1977 - 2011

At the onset of the revolution, the flag of Libya's independence was adopted as the official Libya flag.

Present Day

The same thing happened with the national anthem. My father was watching one of the opposition channels one night when a patriotic song came up, and he immediately lowered the volume. He explained that this song had been the country's national anthem when Libya was a monarchy in 1955 before Qadhafi came to power in 1969. *I do not know Libya,* I thought. I had never questioned what had been before Qadhafi. Libya and Qadhafi were interchangeable to me. It was a highly personalized state, and he ruled every inch of it, so if he was to be deposed, who would we be? What was our national identity away from Qadhafi? Did we know who we were? Those were the questions that ran through my mind that night.

———

The land border to Tunisia remained open, but we could not leave because of our high-profile status. If we went and ran into a checkpoint, my father would be accused of defecting. Besides, my father loved Libya and did not want to leave. There was also the scary possibility of leaving Libya and being unable to return. Nobody knew how long this could go on.

Many people stormed the embassy compound in light of the

NATO operations and defiance of the West for intervening in Libyan affairs. They destroyed it, tore down its walls, and looted everything they could put their hands on. Watching that on the news was surreal. That day, I was literally waiting for someone to come to my house and snatch me. The Americans called me from the States to check on me that day, but I could not pick up. This was uncharted territory. If I answered their sympathetic calls, I knew I would be labeled as a traitor, and I might disappear altogether. My colleagues and I could not call each other either. Nobody wanted to talk about what was going on, and we did not know each other's allegiances. It was dangerous.

After four months, in August, to be exact, I learned that a few of my colleagues had been brought in for questioning that day. I was spared, probably out of respect to my father—who knows?

After the passing of his youngest brother, Mohamed told me that he was planning to cross the border to Tunisia with a few friends for a couple of weeks. I disapproved. What if Qadhafi woke up one day and decided to close the borders and accuse everybody who had left of treason? He would not be able to come back. He said he would not be gone long. In fact, he would be back before I knew it, he reassured me.

That night, after losing count of the falling bombs, I slept with a heavy heart. I woke up around 02:00, checked my phone, and there was a missed call from Mohamed. He had called me a few minutes before I woke up. I dialed him right away, and he picked up. He told me he was about to cross the border and would call me as soon as he got a Tunisian SIM card. He said, 'I called you to let you know that I have known many, many girls in my life, but I have never felt the way I feel when I am with you. You mean so much to me. I love you.'

I was in tears. I said, 'I love you too,' and we hung up.

He started calling from Tunis. We were so much in love it hurt. I had very little money left, but I did not care. I got top-up cards so I could call him, despite how incredibly guilty I felt for spending the money. We talked a lot about us, and he told me how he wanted us to be together, how he wanted to marry me. I was so happy. I started decorating our imaginary home right away. I even gave myself a walk-in closet! Those thoughts kept me going until our next phone call. He would sometimes ask about the bombing, the fuel situation, but we stayed clear from discussing the situation. We did not want that ugliness to touch what we had. We were far more important and way stronger than the shifting sands we were standing on.

I tried reaching him one day, but his phone was out of service. I was confused and worried. He disappeared for over a week, and I got anxious. Then one Friday late afternoon, I received a phone call from an international dialing code. I answered, and it was Mohamed. He was in Jordan!

I was surprised but did not think much of it. We kept on calling each other. We were deeply and strongly in love. He always said that we would never lose each other and that we broke bread together, so to speak. And if the romantic side did not work for whatever reason, we would always remain respectful of each other and in touch.

I was not worried about the romantic dimension. It was amazing, heady, and sublime. My thoughts of him and our imaginary home kept me sane and sustained me in a world of mayhem. His voice tucked me up in bed. I felt reassured and loved.

I started thinking about what to wear when he returned, and I saw him again for the first time. I wanted to paint my nails. Would the hairdressers be open by then? Those silly things kept me alive. It may sound silly or superficial, but that was what I felt. It was my release valve at that time and my escape mechanism.

———

JUNE AND JULY

Weeks followed, May ended, June followed, then July. The temperature was on the rise. NATO became a regular feature of our daily humdrum lives. The novelty of it wore off, and my lethargic existence wore me down. Everybody was waiting for a change, an end to this stalemate. Officials kept on defecting, and cities kept joining the interim government. The front lines kept widening. Tripoli was the destination of the rebels. The regime channels were trying to discredit them and denounce NATO. New TV channels affiliated with the rebels were launched, airing anti-Qadhafi programmes and painting the rebels in a good light. They explained that their main goal was to topple Qadhafi and restore order to Libya, to create the space for civil society to grow and prosper, freedom of speech, free elections—all that was promised, and more. Many people were waiting for those knights to liberate them, to give them the new Libya they had so much desired and dreamt about for years.

Mohamed returned to Tunis, and we chatted the night he was due back in Libya. He was about to cross the border in the morning. I was scared. What if they arrested him? But he was in high spirits. I slept with a smile. When I woke up the next day, I called him, but his phone was off. I thought he was still on the road. I called again: no reply.

The days turned into weeks, and still, there was no sign of him. I called the Tunisian line, the Jordanian line, and the Libyan one; they were all down. My best guess was that he had been arrested on the way back and put in prison. I did not know what to do. There was nothing for me to do. I felt lonely and bereft. I missed him terribly. I became depressed, and I lost my appetite.

My parents' coffee time was reduced to just coffee or tea, no more biscuits and sweets. Most things became a luxury that we could not afford. We needed every penny we had, as we could not access our money. The holy month of Ramadan was fast approaching, due on August 1, and that was another reason we needed all the money we could put aside, so we could buy food while we observed it.

SEVEN
THE BATTLE OF TRIPOLI

AUGUST: 'OPERATION MERMAID DAWN'

August came, with its humidity and uncomfortable heat. We started experiencing something for the first time in our lives—power cuts. I had never thought about electricity before; it was there, like the air or the sky, and one could not help but take it for granted. Now I was made aware of its presence through its absence. First, the power cuts lasted for a couple of hours, and then they began in earnest, lasting up to six or seven hours a day, then eventually 12 or 16 hours a day. There was nothing to do without electricity in this stifling heat. We did not have money for a generator. Sometimes I would lie in bed and stare at the ceiling. I felt less like a dignified human being and more like an animal with every passing day.

According to the media, the date set by the rebels to enter Tripoli was the 20th of August. The operation to enter Tripoli was called 'Operation Mermaid Dawn' as Tripoli was often dubbed 'the Mermaid of the Mediterranean.' We were fasting in the heat and humidity, with no air conditioning due to the power outages. Ramadan is well known for its colourful feasts, family gatherings, and midnight treats, but there was none of that this year. The streets were empty. The shops ran out of goods. That year, we had nothing to break our fast with except lentil soup and mum's bread. Although she was an excellent cook, she was still experimenting with the bread. She had never had to make it at home before. Sometimes it was hard and flavourless; other times, it was hard and salty.

The tradition is to break your fast with milk and dates, eat soup, then eat all the other courses. This year we broke our fast by candlelight, sitting on the floor, gulping the lentil soup, and listening to NATO's soundtrack. To make matters worse, we ran out of cooking gas, and of course, there was none available anywhere. We had coal in the pantry, and we used that. Mum would go outside the kitchen to the backyard, sit on a brick next to the pot, set the coal on fire, and make that soup. Lentil was the only thing we had left; we ran out of supplies.

I stepped outside to help her in the scorching heat and found her hunched over, visibly shrunk, fanning at the fire. That beautiful, elegant lady that all my friends had envied me for was now sitting on a brick, face covered in soot, trying to feed her family. I asked if she needed help, and she smiled and said no. I went to my room crying. It broke my heart to see her like that. I promised myself that if and when things got better, I would take her to a surprise facial at a nice spa, which would be my thank you gift to her. My poor dad would be lying on the floor, fanning himself with a magazine to chase away the summer heat.

It was a matter of time before we ran out of coal. When it finally happened, my poor brother walked outside to cut some branches from the tree outside our house and collect anything that could be used to light a fire. Then, to my horror, the water was cut off. We bought some drinking water and used it for the bathroom, but doing the laundry and the dishes became a distant memory. I was on my period and felt utterly disgusted with myself. It was debasing, a new level of humiliation. I had only one bottle of water to use and could not shower for days. We had a well in the house, but it had always been deactivated as we never needed to use it. Fresh, drinkable water had always been abundant. Finally, after weeks without water, after the rebels had entered Tripoli, we were able to fix the well. I gave all the cash I had stored up to my brother. He found someone who could repair it for us.

In the days leading up to the 20th of August, my father gathered us together and said, 'If the rumours are true, if the rebels have entered Tripoli, then I will stay with your brother outside in the backyard guarding the place, and you will remain in this room and hide. I will lock the doors.'

The night of the 19th witnessed heavy bombardment from NATO. It was clear that they were accelerating the attacks, providing the rebels with the air cover they needed to advance into Tripoli. It was hard without the electricity to verify any information, but you could tell that something was up. We kept the windows open so they would not break. We did not get much sleep that night.

The following day, the rebels indeed entered Tripoli. They took over the HQ of the radio and television station, and the internet was restored. Some figures who went on TV to speak against 'the revolution' were arrested. They went straight to Qadhafi's house, 'Bad Al Azizya,' and found it empty. The rebels walked in, and other people from the neighbourhood also went in. Many looted the place. The prisons were opened. I was anxious. If Mohamed had been in prison all of this time, he would have been out by now. I called his number, but it was still dead.

On the second day, the rebels went to the Green Square; Its original name, 'Martyrs' Square,' was restored. They were celebrating. Many people joined them, happy and relieved at last. Celebratory fires, fireworks, and the new flag, which was the original one, appeared everywhere. The rebels came from most of the cities of Libya, and some were seeing Tripoli for the first time. Free Libya was finally here!

My phone suddenly rang, and it was Mohamed. I wanted to get inside the phone and reach him through it. He said, 'how are you?'

'I am fine. I have missed you. Where have you been?' I replied. 'I've been worried sick about you.'

He said, 'I was with the rebels that entered Tripoli. I was fighting in the frontline all of these past months.'

My love was a rebel! I had mixed feelings about that. I had never suspected anything.

We fixed a date to meet. I, of course, had lost a lot of weight. I tried to find a pair of jeans that would fit me. I went out anxiously, driving for the first time in months. As I was driving, I noticed cobwebs on the side mirrors of my car. I saw heavy machinery. Young guys wearing camo and driving tanks were everywhere.

I entered our usual alley, my eyes searching for him like a bee hunting for nectar. My legs were shaking, and I could feel the pounding of my heart in my throat.

He appeared and signaled me to turn left. I did, and he stood in front of a house. The door was wide open. He had a goatee, looked sun-kissed. He was wearing a white shirt and camouflage trousers, holding a Kalashnikov.

He asked me to go inside the house quickly, so I grabbed my phone and my bag and went in, locking my car on my way. He walked in after me and closed the door, and we went inside the house. My heart was racing. I was behind him, touching his back as he opened the door to a big luxurious living room. I had no idea whose house it was or if the person was still alive.

He leaned his weapon on the wall and grabbed me, and I lunged into him. We hugged so tightly. I can still recall how it felt. He grabbed me and lifted me till my feet no longer touched the ground. He said, 'You have lost weight'; he stared at me, trying to store my image. We kissed and kissed, then collapsed in a heap. I was on top of him, touching his goatee, kissing him, playing with his hair, bathing in his scent. It felt heady and sublime to be in his arms again and know that he was safe and well. And I liked the goatee!

'Why did not you tell me?' I asked.

He said, 'I couldn't. It was supposed to be confidential. I didn't want to harm you in any way. I was thinking about you all the time.'

I was happy and proud of him. He had decided to join the rebels after his brother passed away; he wanted to honour him, to avenge him. I had not wanted him to go down that precarious road, but I could not help but feel proud of him. I respected the fact that he believed in a new Libya, that he wanted a different Libya. That I understood, respected, and admired, despite how differently we viewed our country. We all had different realities and experiences. He was truly happy; he wanted a bright future for Libya. He loved Libya.

———

Out of nowhere, I had this horrible thought: what if the revolution went away, but the feeling of it did not? I mean, I did not feel joy or anticipation. All I could feel was dread. I felt unmoored.

I hoped, against all odds, that things would get back to normal, but they did not. Cash was still an issue because of the sanctions and the frozen assets. Power cuts continued. The water was restored gradually. Colleagues started talking to me. I started calling friends and checking my email. Then I had my first phone call with Chris. He was still in Benghazi. He had been so worried about me the past few months and asked all kinds of questions—how I had coped and what the difficult parts were.

I went back to the same mysterious house for many dates after that. Mohamed took me up a spiral staircase leading to a big bedroom one time. We stole every moment we could to be together. He was becoming busy, and his phone kept on ringing. He was in charge of a battalion, and sometimes they needed guidance on orders. He picked up the phone once and asked them not to harm 'the old man.' He told them that he had spoken to him and given him his word that he would not be arrested. He ordered them to stand down and said he would handle it. After he hung up, he explained that there was an old man who was a supporter of the regime, and the rebels wanted to arrest him, but he was too frail. He would just need to ask him a few questions, no need to terrorize him or his family. But these young guys could get too excited and passionate at times, and they needed someone to control them.

Over the following weeks, we saw a number of public figures being humiliated on TV, having been caught after they spoke against the revolution. Nobody knew all the facts, and nobody wanted the bloodshed. They were not against any revolution; they were merely scared and did not get the full picture. We were all new to this, and nobody could have forestalled it, but the rebels were hasty to act. A few of the men we saw were my father's friends and colleagues. I still shudder to think about what might have been if my father had spoken on television that day.

The following months made it difficult for us to see each other. He was busy stopping any insurgence and trying to stabilise the capital in a security vacuum. Many rebels remained in the city, seeing it as their rightful reward for having sacrificed their lives. In other words, they refused to go back to their home-towns, and that instigated a series of turf wars and frictions between the different rebels, who would later be known as militias.

The embassy called us and said they were coming back. I started going to the office, trying to bring a semblance of normalcy back into my life. We could not go back to the embassy —it had been destroyed—so we started working out of the Ambassador's Residence, while the Americans who came back lived on a compound only a couple of minutes away from it.

Prior to 2011, the diplomats lived scattered across the city; any area was as good and safe as another. They had moved and driven around freely. Now it was different. Security constraints became the 'new normal.' The rebels were everywhere, and they were young; I could not take any risks. I went out only when needed. Many houses were broken into, and families were forced to leave their homes for having had ties with the previous regime. Cars were hijacked. It was dangerous.

The rebels were young and reckless. They were in awe of the capital and the many fancy houses, and they took residence in houses that belonged to members of the previous regime and its entourage. They had no intention of going back, despite the promises they had made. It became a normal occurrence to wake up to an RPG (a rocket-propelled grenade) just because a battalion from a certain city did not agree with another battalion —or they were drunk. Sometimes a group from a certain city wanted to control a certain area of Tripoli. It was a war of leverage and power, and who got the biggest piece of Tripoli.

The more responsibilities Mohamed assumed, the harder it became for us to see each other. I was edgy. I didn't know when he would call to ask me to go out. He was not in control of his time, which made me deeply uncomfortable. He would sometimes call at the most inopportune moments. He was free at night and pleaded with me to spend the nights with him, but that was not possible. I could not just disappear from my parents' house.

———

The Death of Qadhafi

20 Oct 2011

It was a Thursday, and I was at the embassy. Around noon, I heard my colleagues speaking to each other, and suddenly the atmosphere became tense. They were saying that news of Qadhafi's capture was circulating. After many rumours over the course of nine months, you learn to take such news with a pinch of salt, especially since there had been many stories of his escape to live in Latin America, Africa, Russia, and others; I had lost track of how many times his capture had been reported before. My colleagues were nervous and were permitted by management to go home early. They did so. Driving home, I could hear celebratory fires everywhere, men running around the streets, people standing in front of TVs inside the shops watching silently, nervously.

I got home quickly to find my family watching the news,

waiting for confirmation. I went upstairs, sat with my sister in the living room, and watched the news with her. A few minutes later, we saw the graphic footage of Qadhafi's awful, horrendous death. He was captured in his hometown, Sirte. I could not watch the videos. I thought about his family at that moment, who had escaped Libya when the rebels entered Tripoli. I could not imagine what they must be feeling right then.

Nobody in the family talked about that day, probably because of the inhumane way he was killed. My sister and I were silent, watching in disbelief. It was a happy day for some and a sad one for others, but it was an end of an era.

————

NOVEMBER: THE FIRST CUT IS THE DEEPEST

One night I called Mohamed, and a girl picked up his phone. He was fast asleep, drunk. I was heartbroken. He explained the following day that it had been a drunken mistake and it was just sex, but we broke up.

Having never really broken up with anyone before, I did not know what I was supposed to feel. I knew he loved me, but I lacked the maturity to deal with the issue back then. I walked away. The pain was insurmountable, and I did not know how to deal with it. They say people who lose a limb can still feel it there after it is gone. It is called phantom pain. Well, that is how I felt.

————

What happens casually, remains.

— TED HUGHES

One night, I was in bed feeling sad, crying, missing Mohamed. My phone rang. It was James. Let me tell you about James—he was a Geordie lad who was teaching at Newcastle University when I was studying there. We were attracted to each other and went on a few dates; we kissed a few times, but we did not pursue it further as he was leaving to go to another country for a teaching job. He started a relationship there almost right away. We did not stay in touch. That had been years ago, so I was surprised to see him on my screen.

I picked up the phone, and the first thing he said was, 'I cannot believe it, you are still alive.' We chatted a bit. He told me that I had been on his mind all of those months when Libya was in turmoil. 'I wondered if you were okay, but I knew in my heart that you were,' he said. Well, if he was genuinely concerned about me, why could not he call before, I wondered? Friends had called me from all over the world to check on me.

Apparently, he and his girlfriend had parted ways. I honestly thought he was just catching up. The calls continued after that, and he finally came clean and told me what was on his mind. He told me that he had been doing a lot of soul searching and had always felt that he and I had never had proper closure. Now that he was single, he wanted to see if we stood a chance together. He talked about how tired he was with the dating scene and wanted to settle down. He said he had not been able to take his mind off me all those years. I was still heartbroken and naïve, and I believed him. We embarked on an adventure to see if we could be together. Being in two different countries would be challenging, but we would see. Looking back on it now makes me realize how much I have grown and matured since then.

He spoke about how sad and lonely he had been and how his girlfriend had never understood him. I felt sorry for him. We kept talking, night and day. I still missed Mohamed, but I was determined to move on.

Things continued as usual, work and more work, militias fighting each other from time to time, causing disruption, closing off streets. The power cuts persisted.

───────

2012

James and I agreed that we would meet in April in Brussels since I would be there visiting Maria. He explained that he was between jobs and did not have the money to come and see me, so I paid for his ticket to Brussels and the hotels. This would be the first of many, many expensive mistakes.

When we met, he found fault with everything. He did not like the hotel room, so we changed to another one. Then the following day, he decided to change the hotel and the location. Easy for him—I was paying. We moved to an area of his choosing. One of those nights, he gave me his grandmother's ring and asked me to marry him. I was happy initially, but something inside me did not like this. However, I felt compelled to carry on. I showed the ring to Maria, and she was happy for me. He called his ex-girlfriend to tell her the happy news. I thought that was weird, but I did not comment. The next step was for him to come to Libya for the wedding.

One day I decided to open the 'X File.' I asked him how much contact he was having with the ex. He reassured me that their meetings were few and far between and that she was seeing someone as well. I had a feeling that he was not telling the truth, but I ignored it.

I started the paperwork for our marriage. As I was marrying a non-Libyan national, I needed some admin papers before he visited Libya.

Chris Stevens was appointed the Ambassador to Libya, and he arrived in May. It was a lovely reunion. We talked about my 'engagement.' He knew I was not convinced—I could see it in his eyes—but he did not say anything about it.

I know it was hasty on my part, but after the horrible eight months (February-August 2011) when everything I had was gone, my priorities had shifted. I wanted to have something stable and steady, and James seemed like the perfect missing piece of my puzzle. He talked about the wedding and how he would spoil me, sweep me off my feet, and take me to England on our honeymoon. He painted a beautiful picture of marital bliss. I could not wait to marry him. Maybe I would have my 'Kate ending,' like Kate Middleton marrying Prince William—or perhaps I got the signs wrong.

I kept running into Mohamed from time to time. We would look at each other with love and just smile.

'Like two doomed ships that pass in a storm/We had crossed each other's way:

But we made no sign, we said no word, we had no word to say' – Oscar Wilde.

I missed the way he always looked at me like I had something worth seeing. I still loved him, but I could not let myself go back there. I was too fragile for that intensity.

―――――

I have seen war – I hate war.

— FRANKLIN D. ROOSEVELT

Some of the cracks from my traumatic year began to show. I started having nightmares and displaying anxiety and a bad temper. My reactions were out of proportion. Driving to the embassy in the morning, I would see photos on the walls and billboards of young Libyan men who had died, their names, cities, and the date they had passed away. I tried to imagine their stories, aspirations, dreams, the last thing they had thought about before they died, the agony of their mothers. One day I could not drive anymore. I pulled over and cried my heart out.

I had seen James only once in April, in Brussels. After that, we were just talking on the phone. He moved back to England, where he was teaching. He told me he needed to take some time off because he had some difficult times with his former boss and now needed to decompress. Having survived the first chapter of the civil war, I could not honestly relate to that, but I said nothing.

Eight
The fateful night

9/11 Revisited

Chris was getting ready to go to Benghazi, to where it had all started. He had just finished reading a book and lent it to me. It was a novel by Julian Barnes called 'The Sense of an Ending.' That title was very ironic, looking at this now. He could not shut up about it. He asked me to read it fast and give it back to him since he planned to re-read it again after he returned from Benghazi. I gave him a letter written by Beethoven to the object of his affection.

'The Immortal beloved':

> *My thoughts go out to you,*
> *my Immortal Beloved. I can only live wholly with*
> *you or not at all.*
> *Be calm my life, my all. Only by calm considera-*
> *tion of our existence can we achieve our purpose*
> *to live together.*

Oh, continue to love me, never misjudge the most
    faithful heart of your beloved.
Ever Thine
Ever Mine
Ever Ours

Chris loved the letter very much, and we talked a lot about the secret identity of Beethoven's love interest.

Chris went to Benghazi. On September 11, I was in bed, ready to sleep, when my sister came running and knocked on my door. She said, 'wake up, your embassy is under attack!' I jumped out of bed, checking the news. I had thought the attack was here, but I found it was in Benghazi. I called Chris immediately. The phone rang and rang and rang. No answer.

I had a horrible pain in my stomach during that fateful night. I was pacing the living room, calling my colleagues. Nobody knew where Chris was. The eerie darkness of that night is still inside me. It would not leave me. Fear took hold of me like a pillow over my face, stopping me from breathing. I could not sleep. I called Mohamed, crying. He was asleep, but I woke him. He was pleasant to me. We chatted for a few seconds, and he hoped everything would be fine.

I must have slept around 04:00 in the morning of September 12. I woke up with dread and called my colleagues; no news. We had the TV on for any updates. A friend at the British embassy called me to talk about it, and he told me that he had heard some frightening news. I did not ask him; I could not. We hung up.

A few minutes later, I was texting colleagues when I saw big headlines on the screen: AMERICAN AMBASSADOR KILLED IN BENGHAZI. I shouted at the top of my lungs, 'NO!' I rushed downstairs to my mother and collapsed in her lap. I told her, 'Chris died, Chris died!' She could not understand me through all the sobbing. She just patted my head, feeling my pain.

It would be days before I was able to go to the embassy. We were moved to the compound now, with many Marines for protection. I could not stay for the whole day. I just left covered in tears.

The staff was given Chris' villa to work from—were they kidding me? I could not stay there. The kitchen was full of his files, packed. I saw a note with his handwriting on it. I remember how I teased him about his bad handwriting.

There were four who died on that fateful night. I watched on TV as the four coffins were brought back to the States, draped in red, white, and blue. I looked and looked, asking myself which one was Chris. I was utterly inconsolable. Ms. Cecile sent me an email. She was heartbroken.

I could not report to work in the days that followed. I just could not bring myself to move. All the while, the paperwork for my marriage was underway, and I was talking to James. I wanted to cancel everything, but it was too late. Our parents knew, and admin preparations had already begun. I did not want to do it, and I did, in equal measure.

———

OCTOBER

James arrived in October for the wedding. There was no date yet. We were waiting for the approval to come through—slow bureaucracy. As he was between jobs, I had to pay for his ticket and then the flat where he would stay. I had it cleaned and stocked up the fridge for him. I met him at the airport, and we went for a drive around the city. He was comfortable.

The next day, I took him out in the morning to have break-fast, and of course, he started complaining about the quality of service and the food. I tried to explain that we were just rising from the ashes of the war, and some things were not quite what they used to be. He was like a spoiled brat, asking me to drive him around. The sun was intense, and I kept on driving aimlessly, just to please him. Whenever I tried turning on the radio to lighten up the mood with some songs, he would shut it down aggressively.

I took him to O2, where I introduced him to my friends and some Libyan colleagues—the Americans were under lockdown. He had the audacity to ask me one day if I had slept with one of the friends I had introduced him to. I was gobsmacked. Of course not! But I knew he did not believe me.

I still could not go back to the embassy, and my marriage was looming. I needed an extended break to hide away and lick my wounds. I was still processing my breakup, what had happened in Libya, the attack. I could not go on, so I resigned. It was one of the most challenging and painful things I have ever had to do. That chapter of my life was officially over.

James was somehow relieved that I had resigned. He did not like it when I spoke about my colleagues or said how much fun I was having doing my job.

The approval for our marriage came through, so I paid for my wedding dress, the wedding, the catering, and our tickets to England. He promised to take care of me and let me heal and recover. That was all I needed. As for the money, it comes and goes.

My wedding was unremarkable and uneventful. I called Mohamed on my wedding day to tell him. He was outside Tripoli, fighting insurgence in one of the cities. I told him I was getting married today. He said, 'To a foreigner, right?'

'How did you know?' I asked.

'I have seen you two driving around.' I felt my heart drop. He wished me all good things and said he was happy for me.

We spent the first night together in the hotel where the embassy first started. Nothing happened that night; we just went to bed. We went to Newcastle the next day. I guess some things come full circle after all.

NOVEMBER

> There is no better way to know us, than as two wolves, come separately to a wood.
>
> — TED HUGHES

When we arrived in Newcastle, it was cold. We stayed at James's late grandmother's home. Something did not feel right. James was not interested in anything I said. He did not consummate the marriage, and that was terrifying for me. He had a morbid fascination with porn, and as long as he could force me to service him, he had no intention or desire to be with me or connect physically with me. When I tried talking about it, we would fight and not talk for days afterward. Every night he forced me to relieve him, and then he would fall asleep, leaving me to my own devices—the operative word here being 'devices.'

The situation was strange, and I could not talk to anybody about it. My family thought I was with Prince Charming. He did not let me watch my shows or the silly romcoms on the TV in the living room. I started using my laptop for that, and even then, I could not escape his criticism. He criticized my taste in music, films, and clothes. He did not let me leave the house alone. I wanted to go to the theatre, so he made me buy him a ticket so he could go with me. But he was not interested in *The Nutcracker* or *Swan Lake*. He only wanted to control my environment, not share in my interests.

He never let me out of his sight. Even when I wanted to go downtown in the mornings with no specific purpose in mind, he would tag along. We would go everywhere together. Then, at every opportunity he got, he would start criticizing everything I did to the shop assistants in every shop I went into, referring to me as his "Muslim wife," which was humiliating beyond words. One time we were in a Café, and after we had ordered, the shop assistant recommended that we try some of their new selection of sandwiches. He laughed and said, "Well, my Muslim wife here cannot eat pork." Everybody behind us in line was staring at me, and the poor shop assistant did not know how to respond to his insensitive and idiotic remark. This is one of many countless occasions where he put me on the spot because of my religious beliefs or the colour of my skin. His efforts to humiliate me knew no bounds. Yet again, one afternoon, while he was taking a nap, I called my brother to say hello. I guess I was excited to be talking to him and was a bit loud. He woke up angry and demanded to know whom I was talking to, and then said that my annoying Arabic sounds had woken him up. I could go on, but you, dear reader, get the point.

His parents were amazing, lovely people, and they made me feel welcome, but he was strange. I started losing confidence in myself and how I looked. If he did not want to sleep with me, I felt there must be something repulsive about me. I was emotionally drained and exhausted, and he was broken and mean. It was a recipe for disaster.

His ex-girlfriend kept calling him, almost every day, to chat. We were supposed to be on our honeymoon, and she did not respect that. Nor did he. I was spending all my time in the bedroom watching movies and crying. I could not believe what was happening to me.

I asked him to put a stop to the ex-girlfriend, and he refused. He gaslighted me, abused me, and made me question my own sanity. It would be two months before we consummated the marriage, and even after that, there was no sex. He was only interested in using me to please him orally. That was all.

One day, I walked out of the house when it was snowing and ran to a phone booth about a minute's walk from the house. I inserted a bunch of coins and dialed Mohamed. I was sobbing. I told him I was tired and could not take it anymore. He was worried about me and asked me to go back to Libya, but I could not. It would be a scandal if I went back after two months of marriage. It would break my parents' hearts. Against my better judgment, I stayed.

Mohamed messaged me from time to time to check on me. He planned to go to Malta at the beginning of 2013 to study English.

My plan with James was to spend a few months in England to recuperate, then move back to Libya, where I could easily find a job and James could teach English. Of course, he had agreed to that initially, but now he was singing a different tune. He told me that he was not ready to go back to Libya or work and that I should try and find a job in Europe. When I tried to explain that I could not possibly compete in Europe, and besides, I needed to be a resident of an EU country to apply and for my application to be considered, he exploded. He started yelling at me, accusing me of being uncooperative. There was no way of talking to this guy. He almost drove me insane.

Our fights continued, and I grew resentful. He did not care

about me—as long as I had pleased him orally, I could go to hell. My desires and needs did not exist. I did not exist.

I was miserable, and he was miserable. We were like two wounded animals trapped in a cage. It felt like there was a black cloud over the house, full of rage, disappointment, and despair, threatening to rain and drown us in our sadness and sourness. Nothing was right. It was as if I was trying to fit into a dress that was not my size, but I had to because it was the only dress I had, and I did not want to miss the ball. We fought constantly. He brought out the worst in me. I did not like myself around him.

My hair started to fall out, and I got scared every time I washed or brushed it. I was also still grieving for Chris, Libya, my career, my break-up with Mohamed, and my failed marriage. He did not respect that. I often had nightmares and woke up crying. My friends thought I was living the dream, the fairytale. My English Prince had come to my rescue.

———

New Year 2013

We went to James's family house for dinner on New Year's Eve. I wanted to go to the Millennium Bridge for the fireworks at midnight. James did not want to go but felt pressured to pretend in front of his parents and the guests and tell them about our plans for the night. We went back to our place. I was excited to see the fireworks. I had always spent New Year's Eve alone when I was a student here, but this time was different. He kept asking me if I still wanted to go, which dampened my spirits. Around 11:00, I told him that we should get going if we wanted to find a place to park. He said okay, but he needed to call his ex-girlfriend to wish her a Happy New Year. I felt like I had been stabbed with a dagger in my heart. I exploded, and we had a huge fight in which he nearly strangled me. There were no fireworks that night; I cried myself to sleep.

MARCH 2013

> Everything carries me to you, as if everything that exists, aromas, light, metals, were little boats that sail toward those isles of yours that wait for me.
>
> — PABLO NERUDA

I started applying for jobs back in Libya so I would at least be doing something. When James found out, he got angry and asked me why I needed to work. We had agreed that I would rest. It was crazy. I did not understand how he processed things.

My visa was about to run out, so I told him we should go back to Libya and start our new life. He refused and said he would not feel comfortable there. I tried to reason with him and explained that going back to my family's house would be scandalous; people would talk about us. I begged him to be sensitive to my family's name, for my father's sake, but my pleas fell on deaf ears.

I called my mother to tell her that I might be coming back alone. She screamed down the line, 'NO, stay there!' Do not come back alone. When he is ready, you come back together.' I did not know what to do.

So, in a nutshell, he refused to get a job and did not want me to apply for one in Libya. He did not want to go back with me, though he knew I could not stay. And he wanted me to find a job in Europe while he recovered from the 'unpleasant experience' of his former employment.

I decided then and there that this would not work, and I had to get out of there. I traveled back to Libya without telling my parents. I spent a couple of nights at a friend's house and then went to Malta to join my beloved.

———

If you wonder what I felt when I landed in Valletta, Malta—well, you would be mistaken if you think I had butterflies in my stomach. I had an entire zoo in my stomach that day, and the animals had broken out of their cages and were running wild inside me.

The weather was mild and refreshing, a welcome change after the brutal cold of northern England. I was greeted by a gentle breeze that softly kissed my anxious and weary face as I stepped out of the airport. Travelling has always taken its toll on me. I took a taxi and headed to Mohamed's place. I had asked him not to meet me at the airport—I could not possibly handle any more anxiety. Seeing him always had a strong physical impact on me, and I was so frail and traumatized by my marriage that I could not handle the added pressure. Also, there was a good chance that I was looking like crap, and I needed to freshen up at the airport toilets and put on my face before we saw one another.

I boarded the plane looking like my old glamorous self; I disembarked looking like a pile of vegetables that had been left in the fridge for too long. Those romantic airport embrace scenes work better in rom-com movies; it is best to leave them to the silver screen.

So, I got there, and I finally saw him. It felt like we had been brought back to life. Feelings surfaced we had suppressed for a very long time. We embraced, and it was not a Hollywood embrace; it was ours. No soundtrack in the background except our heartbeat and the sound of our kisses. No rolling credits either; this was not the end.

Mohamed's flat was clean, and not because he was expecting me. He had always been a neat guy.

We had an amazing time together, mornings going to cafés and shopping together, nights of boundless pleasure. He slept in my arms every night. I watched him fall asleep, and for a while, I forgot the sorrow and the pain. I wondered if he could taste my sadness when he kissed me.

After two weeks, I went back to Libya, and he followed me a week later.

NINE

THE RETURN OF THE BRIDE

My mother was furious: she did not want me to come back without my husband. But I had nowhere to stay, so I had to come back. I was picked up from the airport and taken straight to my family's house, where I received a lukewarm welcome. I cannot remember if I saw my father upon arrival or not, but I do remember my mother's disapproving face.

It turned out that my parents had packed up the entire contents of my bedroom and turned it into a gym. It was not like I had died; I was only gone for four and a half months. Well, it was good to know that staying in shape was high on their agenda.

I was given a living room with its own kitchen so that I could stay there temporarily—that is, until my 'beloved husband' could join me. My belongings were there, in black trash bags on the floor. It took me days to go through them. I used this opportunity to de-clutter.

My aunt came by the following day to say hello and give me my wedding gift, a soup set. I felt humiliated. I could not talk about what had happened, about the abuse, the ex-girlfriend, the dysfunctional sex. I went to visit my grandmother at the hospital, and she asked if I was pregnant. They all kept asking me about the honeymoon. It was very tense at home. I had gotten married to a man who had come out of nowhere, gone with him to England, and now I had shown up on their doorstep without him. I understood how they felt and how this must have looked, but I was scared and daunted by the magnitude of the problem. I was as lost as Alice in Wonderland. I was so far down the rabbit hole that I could not find my way out. I was a cast-off, a liability that nobody wanted to touch.

I was also broke. I had spent most of my money on the preparations for the wedding, the dress, James's tickets, the rent for the flat he stayed in, and the hotel for our first night as husband and wife, which was a five-star hotel. The spending had not ended when I left Libya; I had spent more and more in England. I had to buy two tickets for every show I wanted to see, so that was an extra burden on my budget, and I wished that he had enjoyed the shows or that they had meant something to him. I paid for groceries. I also had to pay off his credit card debts. One day, he started talking about his debts and that he was thinking about contacting his ex-girlfriend to help him. As they say—for better, for worse—I had no choice but to pay them off myself.

I had to exchange a lot of money to be able to stay in England. One pound was worth 3 LYD in 2013, so if I paid a hundred pounds for something, it meant I had spent this amount three times in my currency. I had tapped deeply and so foolishly into my savings from the moment James walked into my life. I did not see a single dime—or in this case a penny—back from him. I am still resentful and angry, but mostly with myself.

With no job, no prospects, and no money, I had to sell my car for cash. I bought a small second-hand car, cried myself to sleep, and started looking for a job.

My mother was so ashamed that she lied to her friends and told them I was still in England. I found this out by accident when my grandmother died; some of her friends came to the funeral and were surprised to see me there. It was awkward for me, my mother, and her friends. I did not go to the funeral the second day, and I was sure mother was relieved.

I could not go to my aunt's house or see my cousins anymore, as they would start asking me questions, questions for which I still had no answers. When they visited, I hid in my room and pretended not to be there, which was convenient for my family. I could not see my friends either. I was ashamed and in pain, but I could not admit my failure. I did not know what to do or how to cope.

I did not stay in touch with my former colleagues and cut ties with all of them. Ms. Cecile sent me many emails, checking on me and my married life, and I did not answer any of them.

I applied for a job with an International Organization, and I got it. After examining my experience with the embassy and the recent unfortunate events I had gone through, I needed something away from my life. I decided to keep my job separate from my life. I wanted a job that I could manage instead of one that consumed my very existence.

I started reporting to the office and made sure that I was not overinvested in the job. I kept my colleagues at bay and hardly said a word about myself and my life. It was a low-profile job, an office job—no receptions, no mingling. It was what I needed. I wanted to fade into the background.

I wanted to introduce the topic of divorce to my parents, but I just did not have the courage. It was too early for that. It sounded like a huge deal, and I was thinking about the family, our reputation, and the neighbours. If my mum had to lie to save face, they would never accept the idea of my divorce.

The longer I stayed, the more apparent it became that I was not thinking about going back to England or that James planned on coming to Libya. My marriage became the big elephant in the room. Everybody was tiptoeing around it. Nobody wanted to address it. Nobody cared to know about my pain, my suffering, the loss of my money, as long as I kept a lid on it.

To start generating more cash, I went back to the school where I had given the English courses when I first got back from England. I left the office around 16:30–17:00 and was at the school before 18:00. My classes were from 18:00–20:00, and I arrived home around 20:30 if I did not see Mohamed—around 21:00 if I did see him, but either way, I went straight to my room. I escaped.

Those were dark times. The school and thoughts of Mohamed were the only two things that brightened my day. I loved teaching. I could see my students' progress and how they understood the grammar and used it correctly. They did not speak a word of English initially, but by the time I was done with them, they could converse with me in English. I invested a lot in those courses. I designed my own material, in addition to the curriculum I was required to give. The students loved me and often brought me gifts. They were a source of healing, though they did not know it. I also met some lovely teachers. It was a very pleasant experience.

But Libya continued its downward spiral. Prices were on the increase. There were assassinations, kidnappings, forced disappearances, power cuts, cash, and fuel shortages, along with many other issues. The once-celebrated rebels had transformed into beasts, bringing the capital to its knees. Some diplomatic missions had resumed operations from Libya in 2012, but with restrictions regarding the number of personnel allowed on the ground. However, after the attack on the US consulate, the deterioration of the security situation, and the heavy-armed presence in the capital, it was not practical anymore to work from Libya. It was just a matter of time before all missions evacuated from Libya to start operating from Tunisia.

As the stage for many battlefields of various militias, the capital was put under enormous pressure. Electricity and water were used as leverage in negotiations if a particular militia was at odds with another in Tripoli or a militia in Tripoli had kidnapped someone whose tribe was from the south. The south could easily cut off the water supply to the entire capital (almost two million citizens), as the pumping stations were there until their demands were met. These issues occurred frequently and worsened in the heat of the cruel Libyan summer.

Power stations were often vandalized. They became a vital target for warring parties and had been repeatedly hit since 2011. Ground cables and copper wires were stolen, resulting in massive blackouts, plunging the capital into darkness. Sometimes we got the electricity back for two or three hours. There was no schedule for the outage, so you were left on your toes the whole time, running around frantically to try to do your chores before the power went off again. I had to do my ironing for an entire week in one go. Beads of sweat would roll down by back from the scorching heat. You needed a schedule for the laundry as everybody in the family would be waiting with a basket full of dirty clothes. The sounds of generators punctuated our summers instead of the sound of the waves. We could not afford to buy one; they became ridiculously expensive. Food spoiled, and household appliances broke down from the unstable current due to vandalism. Many families, mine included, had to buy a new air conditioner, a freezer, or a TV at one point or another. I used the office to charge my phone and personal laptop many times. I even had to shower at work a few times when the water was cut off.

Imagine being this helpless and hopeless and having no right to dream or live. You woke up without electricity or water, drenched in sweat. You could not have your morning shower. It was humid, sticky, and disgusting, especially if you were a woman and on your period—no water even to flush your blood away. Cats are luckier than us in that regard; sand was always available in abundance. Tell me, how can you face the world with a day like that, when you have to go out and start queuing for bread, for petrol, for the little cash you were allowed to withdraw? I had so many of those days.

I started going to the Turkish bath every Saturday to get clean and wash the misery of the city off me. I would slather some soap all over my body and lie there on the hot bench in the steaming room, let everything fall off me and shedding those memories, like a snake shedding its skin. There was a time I had to queue for five hours in the heat to refill my gas tank and a time when I kept driving to find a secure way home to avoid checkpoints. I envisioned all of those experiences going away, leaving my body with the soap. I left the bath reborn, clean, a human being again.

I still felt my love for Libya in the middle of it all. I had always assumed that I loved my country, as there was no way to think. But after going through all of that, I realised I did love her the way mothers love a sickly child. They always love them a little bit more, in spite of everything. After seeing how Libya was like a gazelle being repeatedly ripped to shreds by a pack of wolves, I loved her.

Seeing Mohamed was not always easy, as I have explained. He was now staying at a villa, and as luck would have it, it was in the same spot—our alley. The house had once belonged to one of the senior officials in the previous regime, and he only occupied one room, on the ground floor, with a huge bed on the floor that dominated the room. There was a TV there and a lot of DVDs. That room became our safe haven, where the outside ugliness could not touch us. We watched movies, took naps together, told each other jokes.

Before our dates, I had to blow-dry my hair. I am not lucky enough to just shower and go out, as my hair would resemble cotton candy. I needed to make it presentable, but going to the hairdresser was a cumbersome task. First, if the power was out, I could not go to a nearby hairdresser because it would not have electricity. It would also mean that I had to drive around to find a hairdresser that was open and had electricity or a generator. Sometimes I would find one with a generator, but it was not on, as it was too early in the day to plug it in. And if you were looking at 12–13 hours without electricity, the generator would die at the peak time of day. They would not just plug it in on my account; they needed to save it for wedding reservations. It was frustrating to drive around in the stifling heat, keeping an eye on my petrol tank with my boyfriend calling me and asking me to hurry as he was not always sure of his schedule. It was maddening.

Towards the end of 2013, all the warning signs were there: something very ominous and defining was going to happen in Tripoli. I had developed my radar by then, and I did not deny reality the way I had in 2011.

TEN

THE PENDULUM SWINGS

2014

I was like a glass filled to the brim with water and placed on an unsteady table. I could not apply for a spouse visa, as that would have required James to have a job and an active bank account, neither of which he possessed. I imagined Ms. Cecile in my room, looking at me as I ignored her emails. I felt guilty. I hoped she could forgive me one day.

My new colleagues asked me a few questions about my life, and of course, it was far easier and simpler just to tell them I was married, but they did not stop there. They wanted to dig for more details. I had to lie and invent a postcode for my husband and me and say we were both living there, though I hated myself for doing so. I was burdened down by my story. It felt like I was hiding a body that had started to decompose, and everybody started to smell the stench. I could not embrace my story. I could not own it. It was too heavy for me to carry. I realised many years later that you could not avoid pain by running away from it. You have to stare it in the eye.

I suppose I should let you draw your own conclusion about why I had decided to get married, but let me explain my side of the narrative. By the time James contacted me, I had already reached the end of my tether. I was in a fragile state of mind. My decision to get married was irrational at best, suicidal at worst. It was certainly a financial suicide.

My financial situation had now gotten better, and the school paid me in cash, which meant I always had money. One day in 2015, I tried calling Mohamed, but his phone was switched off. He then called me from a different number to let me know that this phone had been stolen. He had spent the night in one of those military compounds that belonged to his brigade, and that was when it had been taken. He was sad about it as it was a gift from a friend.

I thought about buying him the exact same iPhone, so I did. I put it in a lovely gift box and put a long-stemmed red rose with it. We were supposed to meet two days later. I waited impatiently for our date, and when it finally arrived, I gave him the box and the rose. He opened the box and saw the phone: he was speechless. He was deeply touched by the thought. He told me later that he had almost cried when he saw it. I still remember the look on his face: it was humbled, happy and grateful. We had a wonderful evening.

A few days after that, we met one morning. He put me in bed and slipped out of the bedroom. He came back a few seconds later with a huge bouquet of flowers in a reciprocal gesture. It was his way of thanking me. Flowers were all he could get me, but I loved the gesture. It was so sweet, genuine, and innocent. I fell in love with him a little more deeply that day, just when I had thought that was not possible anymore. I took a picture of the flowers when I got home to cherish the memory.

I had tried to call James to find a way to end our marriage, but every time we talked, it degenerated quickly. He blamed me for everything. I think he would have blamed me for the Irish potato famine if he could have. He called me names, told me I was unhinged and bipolar. I never go through manic episodes, and I sleep at 22:00 every night—how could I have been bipolar?

———

One thing that annoyed me during my dates with Mohamed was the constant phone calls. His phone rang all the time with people asking him for help. They had different stories: someone in hospital who needed help, someone whose brother had been kidnapped by a militia, someone who wanted a new passport to travel. Everyone had a story, and he helped each and every one of them. He prioritized those calls ahead of our relationship. He woke up early in the morning to help people. He stood by them, people he did not know. It was enough for him that they had sought his help. He was a generous man. He did not have much money, but he had a generous and beautiful soul. Being in one of the biggest brigades gave him access, connections, and leverage to help people. He became very powerful over the years. He rose to fame and became the second-in-command in that brigade, but he remained the same guy. He did not change. He helped many displaced people to go back to their homes. He protected the properties of many people in his neighbourhood when they fled the raging war. He was a man I admired immensely.

Being famous created some issues for us. We had to be extra discreet in meeting up so I would not be linked to him. He would often be featured in some news item or other. My heart smiled every time I heard friends and family talking highly about him—they did not know about us. He was likened online to a brave lion or great hero, but to me, he will always be the guy I saw at the corner of the street who captivated me, body and soul, the one who fell asleep in my arms.

In Libya, we were no better off than the previous year. We were still trapped inside this house of mirrors and could not find the exit. The same issues of power cuts and instability persisted. Since 2011, the country had been plunged into chaos. Some militias had more weight than others, depending on how much they had contributed to the revolution and what places they controlled in Tripoli. One of those was a faction that controlled Tripoli International Airport.

The warning bells rang like bells in a monastery, awakening our deepest and worst fears. Libyans were holding their breath, trying to get off the Ferris wheel. In August 2012, the National Transitional Council, formed at the beginning of the Libyan uprising in February 2011, handed over power to the General National Congress (GNC), which came to power after the first and only successful Libyan election in 2012. However, the election failed to create a strong government that could exert its power over the Libyan terrain or control the militias established in the wake of the revolution and entering Tripoli. The GNC was attacked in 2013 many times by armed groups. They stormed the assembly hall and kidnapped many of the members. Some militias saw it as their right to stay in Tripoli and rule it after taking part in the revolution. It was payback time.

The GNC set Jun 2014 as the date for elections to the House of Representatives. The election was held, but due to the security situation and the declining enthusiasm of the public, the voting turnout was low. Nevertheless, despite the disrupted election, the House of Representatives became a legislative body in August 2014, and it replaced the GNC. Islamists groups who lost the election accused the House of Representatives of being dominated by those sympathetic towards the old regime and continued to support the old GNC. The HOR faced many threats and incidents that disrupted its sessions and stopped them from convening or completing.

On a parallel narrative in the East, many terrorist groups found a breeding ground in Benghazi after the attack on the American Consulate. They carried out a number of assassinations of human rights activists and journalists. In May, a Gadhafi-era defector, General Haftar, came back from exile and launched 'Operation Dignity' in Benghazi to purge it from the terrorist and Islamist groups. He called on militias in Tripoli to ally their forces with his. One of the most powerful militias in Tripoli, the one in control of Tripoli International Airport, did so. Soon discord and distrust grew between the various ranks. Driven by a desire to protect their interests in the capital, many armed forces in Tripoli formed an alliance to drive that militia out of Tripoli, defend their interests in the city, and correct the path of the revolution. In July 2014, they launched 'Operation Libya Dawn.'

Eleven

Operation Libya Dawn

Former Comrades of Yesterday are Today's Enemies

On the night of July 13, 2014, during Ramadan, we heard loud shelling. We all emerged from our bedrooms and met with panic on our faces. The sound grew heavier and louder as the night wore on. The militia was strategically stationed at Tripoli International Airport and its vicinity. Libya Dawn forces were firing rockets from a distance; those rockets were met with more rockets. Many people living in the surrounding areas had to leave their homes. I could not go to the office or school anymore.

It was a continuous bombardment. We could not sleep anymore. We slept when the rebels slept, which was the early hours of the morning, and we woke up with them around noon. Many innocent civilians died. They were the worst clashes I had witnessed to date.

From following up the news, I gathered that Mohamed's brigade was going to join Libya Dawn. I was terrified; I did not want him to fight. I escaped one night after breaking the fast to see him. I told mum that I needed to buy sanitary towels as things were deteriorating quickly, and soon, I would not be able to find any.

As I drove, I was listening to the Coldplay song 'A Sky Full of Stars,' thinking Mohamed was my sky and my stars. The irony was not lost on me that night: It was more like a sky full of rockets, not stars.

I got into the house, and we jumped on his unmade bed, kissing and hugging. We made love, all the while hearing the rockets falling on our beloved city. He opened the window so it would not break, letting the moonlight in, crawling upon his skin. I kissed it. I kissed the moonlight.

I asked him if he was going to join the battle. He looked away, smiled, then grabbed me and kissed me.

I was scared about driving back. The streets were empty and dark. No electricity, just shelling and more shelling. I had missed calls from my mother, my brother. I had to rush back.

The rockets continued to land randomly, and then they started landing at the airport. Within a day or two, the airports and the planes were destroyed completely. The UN mission evacuated its personnel by land soon after.

One morning, we were awoken to the sound of a rocket falling on our neighbour's house, destroying its top floors. The house was four houses down from ours. The sound of the rocket still rings in my ears to this day. My siblings and I rushed downstairs; after the first hit, we were waiting for the second one. I don't know if it was seconds or minutes, but we were there in our dressing gowns, feeling helpless, waiting to die. There was nowhere to hide. My brother was so scared that he collapsed on the floor in a desperate attempt to hide underneath the marble. He was repeating 'shhh, shhh, do not speak, do not speak,' as if that would make a difference. He was trying to get a sense of control over something. I was afraid to go to the toilet that day, in case a rocket fell on me. To this day, I still do not know how that rocket came to fall on our neighbour's house, but I am so grateful that the second hit we waited for never came.

The shelling was incessant; it literally did not stop. My mother and brother had a meltdown. They were the first to collapse—the first, that is, if I do not count my sister, the drama queen. She was in a league of her own. I had to remain silent and composed for them, but when I retreated to my bedroom, I cried. We were all resigned.

The second day, the shelling was near. My father told us we had to leave. 'Leave our house?' I asked. He said, 'No. The city'. He asked us to pack the essentials. I packed my toiletries and a pair of pyjamas and a book, 'A House in the Sky,' a memoir by Amanda Lindhout. The memoir detailed her harrowing experience of being kept hostage in Somalia.

I called Mohamed that night to tell him. He said the roads towards the west were fine, and I should let him know once I had arrived safely. He also told me he would be joining the fighting. My heart sank.

We were to leave at the break of dawn—I probably should not say 'dawn' anymore. We were so scared of leaving our house, and what if someone recognised my father and decided to cause us trouble? We were all up around 06:00. It was the first of August. My mother took the meat from the fridge and put it outside the house for the cats. I wanted to eat something but could not. I had some tea with milk and biscuits, but I left them at the bedside table. We took the deeds of the house and left everything else. We could not take anything of value with us in case we were searched at a checkpoint. We took two cars: my brother and myself in one car, my parents and sister in another.

The morning was quiet, and we snuck out like thieves. We had no plans—none. We just could not stay there anymore.

We took the highway towards Zawiya, 45km west of Tripoli. There were no checkpoints in sight. To our surprise, there were many, many cars driving the same way, and they all had belongings with them. I saw their sheets, suitcases in the cars, with kids on top of each other. It was comforting and heartbreaking in equal measures.

When we reached the outskirts of Zawiya, we found a big sign that read 'Zawiya welcomes the residents of Tripoli.' I burst into tears when I read it. There were several young guys with cans of petrol, asking if we had enough petrol to reach our destination.

When we reached the centre, it turned out that there were many people from Tripoli staying there as IDPs, 'Internally Displaced People.' They saw my father and immediately took him to the committee that handled all the issues of IDPs. The committee was based in a school, and there were many people from the city there offering their houses for the IPDs. We were given a house free of charge, one of many on a farm that belonged to a family, and they were happy to welcome us.

We drove to the farm, and they let us stay in a big villa. I felt relieved but strange to be in someone else's home. They made us a hearty breakfast. I still remember that breakfast. It was always my dream to have all my family together, gathered around for breakfast, and finally, I got my wish. They made sandwiches for us and poured our tea and coffee. They were extremely nice. I felt humbled. They were fans of my father, and they could not believe that they were hosting him.

The farm had cows; it was weird to hear them mooing. It was so quiet there, no cars, no city noises. Around lunchtime, they sent us lunch: it was a yummy traditional Libyan meal. I just could not believe it. My faith in humanity was restored. A lot of feelings that I did not understand filled my heart. We all slept soundly that night.

The family had two daughters, the elder one at university and the little one in primary school. The wife was a teacher, and the husband was a businessman. When we woke up the next day, we found breakfast at our doorstep. It was something that only fairies would do. They invited us to their house in the evening for formal introductions.

We kept on following the news, and my brother would call one of the neighbours to go around and make sure the house did not show any sign of forced entry.

There was no shelling in Zawiya, as the city's armed groups were fighting in Tripoli. They were part of Libya Dawn operation. There were no power cuts either. It was normal.

After a few days, when the horror of the past week had been processed, I started reading the book I had brought with me, 'A House in the Sky.' It was so relevant.

Our hostess would organise evenings on the farm and invite all the women in the area to meet us. We would all sit together, drink tea, and exchange stories from the days of 2011. We went to the beach with them a couple of times, and it was such a delight. I had not been able to go to the beach since 2010, as militias had been staying in some of those nice resorts, and we just could not enjoy summers anymore. We had to survive; there was no time for us to think about going to the beach.

One day, I took my brother's car and went out with my mother to the shops. We wanted to buy some biscuits and ice cream. We were talking to each other in the shop when the shopkeeper detected our accent. He said, 'you came from Tripoli, right?' We responded 'yes.' He then refused to take money for anything and told us that anything we wanted would be on the house. People felt our pain. Everybody knew what Tripoli had been going through.

I called Mohamed from time to time, often in the evenings. He did not always respond, and when he did, it felt like he was in a control room. I could hear radios in the background.

I had a really good time in Zawiya, but sometimes, out of nowhere, I would be gripped by those uncharitable thoughts: what if we could not go back anymore? What if our house got broken into? What if they blocked the coastal road?

By mid-August, my family was growing restless. My mother was tired of socialising and came up with excuses to avoid the evening gatherings. On August 23, the airport was captured by Libya Dawn forces, and subsequently, that militia was driven out of the capital. We were so relieved, not because we sided with one party, but because it meant we could go back home to Tripoli.

We were happy but anxious. Going back needed planning. The coastal road had been closed, which meant we would have to drive through a town notorious for looting and criminal activities. We decided to give it another week to see which way the wind was blowing, and we decided to go back on September 1st.

Saying goodbye to that wonderful family was hard. Their little girl hid in her room, crying. She begged us to stay, and we promised them we would come back and visit. It was a promise made in all sincerity, but it was not meant to be. We bought them some parting gifts with the bit of cash we had: a tea set and a vase. We cleaned the house that night and left first thing in the morning. I will always remember that city and its wonderful people warmly. I felt my heart overflowing with an overwhelming emotion: gratitude.

We kept on driving in a very long line of cars, all honking and waving to each other. Everybody was happy to be going home. We ran into many checkpoints where they stopped cars, opened their boots, and ushered them to drive on. As we drove past several guys standing by, we were like a caravan with the other cars, and we felt protected. They started shouting, 'Go back to Libya Dawn, hurry, hurry, living under the thumbs of militias.' My brother and I kept a straight face, looking ahead of us. We did not move. I am sure we did not breathe even until we were far from them.

I was chatting with my brother and relaxing when he looked in the rear-view mirror and realized he could not see my father's car. He said, 'He must have been recognized.' He called my mother, and she answered, crying. She said, 'We were stopped.' We pulled to the right until the cars passed us, then we swerved back, looking for their vehicle. We finally spotted it. My father was standing next to one man while another had the entire contents of the boot emptied and on the ground. They had spotted my father and thought they would scare him. They told him they were looking for weapons. They finished searching, then sent us on our way. It was just a power play.

As we entered Tripoli, I rolled down the window and stretched my arm out as if to touch the city. My father's car was in front of us, and I saw my sister doing exactly the same thing simultaneously. It was like looking in a mirror.

When we got home, I walked into my bedroom and found my cup of tea and the biscuits still there. I immediately started cleaning the house. It was so good to be back.

After this, the front lines moved towards Zawiya, chasing some militias affiliated with Dignity Operations, and Mohamed went there with them.

OCTOBER 2014

Since my office had been evacuated, I started teaching full-time at the school from 10:00–20:00 straight. I still checked my work email and worked when needed, but I was not of much use remotely, and I did not mind. I wanted to teach.

I was worried about Mohamed. We chatted when he could. I missed him terribly. Sometimes I would be driving, and for a split second, I would see him in a stranger's face, even though this stranger bore no resemblance to him, but I missed him so much my mind wanted desperately to conjure him up. So I waited; I waited for him to come home safely. '

> So I wait for you like a lonely house, till you will see me again and live in me. Till then my windows ache.

> — PABLO NERUDA

TWELVE
A Tale of Two Governments

The Tripoli-based Libya Supreme Constitutional Court ruled on 6 November 2014 that the House of Representatives elections that had taken place in June were unconstitutional. The House of Representatives rejected the verdict, saying that it had been coerced 'at gunpoint'. Former members of the dissolved body of the GNC reconvened and declared themselves a replacement of the elected HOR. Consequently, the HOR had to relocate to the east of the country, aligning itself with General Haftar—so the country now had two governments.

Libya Dawn had plunged us into darkness. Everybody was still reeling from the war, barely able to keep up with the ongoing issues. As autumn came, the city slowly returned to life, but it was never the same. Everybody was on edge. We were all waiting for the next blow. Many people had lost their homes and livelihoods. My friends had lost their jobs when their companies evacuated from Libya.

A capital without an airport—can you imagine? The capital

had another airport that was used to receive military delegations and dignitaries under the former regime days, and this was now re-opened. Still, no other airlines were coming in, only our Libyan companies flying in and out. It was too risky to fly over our dangerous skies. There were no destinations or routes except for Tunisia and later Turkey and Egypt. If you needed to go anywhere else, you had to connect via those countries.

By that time, my passport had expired, but I was so plunged into despair that I did not even want another one. I just could not see the point. I was so far removed from my former self, partying in Nice and Monaco. Where did she go? I was disappearing, and I did not care. I was emotionally drained.

My office contacted me from Tunisia, asking if I could join them and work from there, but I could not go. I did not want to get a new passport. I felt shackled and weighed down by everything and could not break free. The Stockholm syndrome, perhaps? I spent my entire time at the school. It was my sanctuary in the cold. I wanted to do something good, leave a positive mark in someone's life.

At the end of November, Mohamed came back. I left the house very early on a rainy morning to get breakfast from O2 and took it to his place. I woke him up with coffee, pancakes, and sandwiches, and we spent the entire morning in bed, listening to the rain. It was dark and cosy, completely cut off from the outside.

We watched a movie, 'American Sniper,' about a US Navy SEAL sniper coming back home and being unable to adjust to his former life. My head rested on Mohamed's chest as we watched the movie, and it was heartbreaking how relevant it was. He spoke after the film about his comrades who fought with him and how difficult it had been for them to re-adjust to reality after the horror of wars and burying their friends. I wondered how much he was carrying around with him, how much of the war had touched or changed in him. I could not feel any difference or see any changes, but he was a human after all, and I was in love.

———

2015-2016: STALEMATE

The following year, 2015, brought the same uncertainties and anxieties. Nothing got better, and there was no hope for us in sight. Nobody could tame the militias, and their frequent skirmishes were just another Tuesday for us. Any attempt at a political dialogue died at conception.

I remained in Libya, teaching at the school and remaining available for my office back in Tunis. I still refused their invitation to join them in Tunisia, and I was still without a passport. The acute cash liquidity shortage reached its worst in 2015, and if it had not been for the school paying me in cash, I would not have had a single dinar to spend. Being the only one in the family who was in possession of cash, I started supporting them, paying for groceries and whatever was needed around the house.

My relationship with Mohamed remained the same, strong and passionate, and I kept falling more deeply in love with him. We had endured a lot together as a couple, as Libyans living in Libya and separately as individuals. We had survived wars, infidelities, marriage, the deaths of siblings and friends, and much more, but we had always found our way back to each other. It was a modern fairy tale.

When 2016 came, my office deemed it safe enough for the national staff to start reporting from the office for a few hours every day, so I had to cut back on my courses at the school. I went to the office in the mornings and then to the school in the evenings.

One day when I was at work, Mohamed called me. He told me that I had been on his mind all night and wanted to see me *now*. He begged me to leave work, and I said I could not, but he insisted. Finally, I yielded and left. It was the rush hour. He kept ringing me the whole time, checking where I was. When I arrived, I was trying to remember what kind of underwear I had on that day, hoping it was decent enough.

He was waiting for me in his car, so I left my car and rode in his. He said, 'I miss you.' He took me to a different house, but in the same area. As we entered, he was holding my hand the whole time. We went to the bedroom, and he lifted me and threw me on the bed, then got on top of me, and we made love. He fell asleep in my arms.

I wanted to leave to get to school, but I could not move as he was sound asleep, so I stayed until I dozed off. We woke up at dusk. We forgot where we had left my car, but eventually, we found it, and he dropped me off. I went home, and he went out with his friends.

If you were wondering by now what had happened with my marriage, well, technically, I was still married. James and I had not talked in almost three years. I knew what needed to be done; I just needed time to get there. And courage.

———

Frankenstein in the Neighbourhood

The turf dance the Frankenstein militias had performed to perfection over the years was far from over. The monster now wanted to occupy the vital site of our neighbourhood, an affluent neighbourhood along the coast. That put a mark on Mohamed's back, as he became unofficially in charge of neighbourhood safety.

Their manoeuvres started by sneaking into the neighbourhood at night and shooting to terrorize the neighbours and provoke them. The battalion safeguarding the area had no choice but to engage. Everything would go back to normal in the morning, but then at night, the shelling re-started. The situation continued for almost two weeks until one night; they broke into Mohamed's house when he was asleep. Miraculously, he managed to escape by the skin of his teeth. He could not go back to the area, so he remained in hiding.

The militias that took over patrolled the streets drove recklessly and, stationed checkpoints. A vacuum was created when Mohamed left, and his absence was taken advantage of. Many feared him and did not dare go into the area, but the word of his disappearance spread like fire. Looters and gangsters roamed the streets. Carjacking incidents were reported and petty thefts. The once trendy area became deserted.

This was a new reality for us. We could not meet there anymore; it was dangerous for him and me if they caught wind of whom he was dating. They could easily use me as leverage. We just talked on the phone.

———

ESCAPADES WITH A FUGITIVE

One morning, I was awakened by my buzzing phone. It was coming up to 06:00. It was Mohamed. He told me he was on his way to see me and I should be up and out in less than five minutes. He could not lurk around in the area in case someone saw him. His friend was staying in the house which was our usual meeting place.

I jumped out of bed and showered in a couple of minutes. He kept calling and calling, urging me to hurry and saying they would get him if they knew.

When I arrived, Mohamed was standing outside the garage with his friend. He opened the garage doors wide, and I drove in. His friend walked inside the house before me, giving me space. As we looked around the room, we found out that much of his stuff— the gifts I had given him for his birthday that year, some of his clothes —had been stolen by the militias that had stormed the house that night: I was sad; I had put a lot of thought into preparing his birthday gifts. But then it dawned on me that they had taken more from me than that. They had stolen my sense of calm, my best years, and my freedom. What if they had taken some gifts? We had each other.

Mohamed told me that when he had called his friend to let him know he was coming over, his friend had asked him if he was out of his mind. He disapproved of him coming back to the area and told him that he would be killed if this was discovered.

'You are worth risking my life for,' he said, kissing me. I kissed him back, rearranging his wild hair, and we made love, tender love. He told me so many sweet and beautiful things until he fell asleep. Those things will forever stay with me, buried in my heart. He was a calming force and a constant presence in my life. He was my anchor, my Libya.

We fell asleep for a couple of hours. He said he needed to leave before everybody was up. He took my heart with him that morning. I could not do anything that day. My body and soul soared high up between the clouds, and I could not come back to reality. I relived the morning in my head over and over until I fell asleep.

Now I began to worry about him. I spent hours combing social media, trying to learn more about his situation and find out if the militias were willing to negotiate.

Weeks turned into months as he remained in hiding, but he kept taking terrible risks to see me. He called me one day at around 06:00 and again asked me to be ready in a few minutes. He was coming to take me with him. One of his friends drove him.

He got out of his car, leaned on my window, and asked me to move over. He was going to drive. He drove my car, listening to Adele on the radio. The drive was a long one, so I knew the place must be on the outskirts of Tripoli.

Finally, we entered a very big, luxurious compound, which must have been a guesthouse for an oil company or an embassy. There were many villas and swimming pools—it was picturesque. He parked, and we entered the villa. His friend followed us into the compound a few seconds after us. There were some guys a fair distance away.

We walked into the villa and went to the bedroom. I was sleepy and hungry, and dizzy. He sat on the bed and brought me closer. He held my hands and looked into my eyes.

'I have missed you,' he said. I was happy to be in his arms but worried about what lay ahead. The militia had taken over the neighbourhood, and I knew it was only a matter of time before there was a counter-attack to get them out of there. I did not want him to fight. I did not want to lose him.

We made love. We merged into one another; I did not know where his body ended, and mine began. Over the years, his body had become like a map of a battlefield. His scars were like unmarked graves of fallen soldiers. His body was like a battlefield graveyard where his comrades and memories of past combats were interred. I would trace them with my fingers, feel them, and with time I memorized them. I could find them with my eyes closed. I did not ask about their stories, though.

He fell asleep, but I did not. I was so tired, but I could not sleep. I checked my phone and found two missed calls from my HR colleague. I sent him a message saying I was sick and could not go to the office. Then I texted one of my best friends, a young guy, Sidig. We had met at an exhibition for the French Institute in 2010 and had been friends ever since. He often confided in me about his crushes, seeking my insights on the female psyche and the ever so beguiling female world. I asked him to guess where I was, and he had no idea, so I told him. He was happy for me. Then I offered to share the intimate details of what happened, and he said, 'spare me. I love you, you are my best friend, but that is the kind of thing you keep to yourself'. So we ended our chat, and I put the phone back in my bag.

I got bored, so I walked out of the room and took a look around the villa. I found a bookshelf with one book, and to my surprise, it was the collected works of Pablo Neruda. I got the book, went back to bed, and read until he woke up.

We cooked pasta and ate together. If we had waited any longer to eat, I might have fainted. We watched some silly TV shows and talked about us, and then it was time for me to leave before my car turned into a pumpkin. We left the same way we came—him driving my car and his friend driving his. He drove me until we reached a point where I would know how to get home. He got out of my car, and I jumped into the driver's seat. He kissed me and asked me to call him once I got home, then went with his friend.

It was a struggle to see him after that. We often agreed to

meet, then something urgent at work would require his attention, and he would call and cancel. Sometimes I would be on my way to see him. It was so frustrating that it reached the point where I had no more tears to cry.

Thirteen

Anchors Aweigh

My boss in Tunis was making waves about how much he needed support and saying it was difficult working with me remotely. I smelled trouble, so I inquired, and it turned out that he had been vetting some people for my replacement, someone to stay in Tunis and do my job while I got tucked away nicely on a shelf.

We had an office retreat in Tunis coming up in October, so I asked my father to use his connections to help me get a new passport. I had tried to do it without his help, but the waiting list in the system was over a year. My father got me an appointment; someone accessed the system and put my name there. I went the next day for my biometrics, and the following day someone delivered my passport to our house.

I got ready for the trip and made a plan. I was nervous the night before, as I had not been to the airport since the main one was destroyed. I had no idea how the militias were running it. I did not want to provoke or attract unwanted attention, so I wore baggy clothes, no makeup, my hair pulled back. When I got there, it was full of families and girls on their own. I felt comfortable, though you could see guys dressed in camo walking around. I thought if I remained calm and made no eye contact, I would be fine.

I got to the customs and handed in my passport. The officer eyed me up, identifying me from my passport photo. He asked who had dropped me off. I wanted to say, 'seriously, did you actually think I would let the object of my affection see me looking like this?' But that would have been a stupid question. I said, 'my brother did.' He stamped my passport, and just like that, I was free. It would be my first time out of Libya since 2013 and my first time in Tunisia.

I had always heard positive feedback on Tunisia, but I had kind of put a pin in it. I did not know what to expect. So when I got there, I was shocked to my very core. Tunisia was a beautiful country. A very modern capital with great infrastructure. Colourful nightlife, with nightclubs and discos. It was hard to imagine this was going on right next door to us. We were so close, yet worlds apart.

What struck me most was how normal life was. I had thought the Tunisians would be suffering like us since they had gone through the transition. In fact, it was they who had lit the first torch. Their country was still a country, while ours had a weak government, flawed institutions, and decaying infrastructure. Libya, prior to 2011, was a deeply personalized state, so with Qadhafi out of the equation, it in effect ceased to exist.

Seeing people out and about with not a care in the world broke my heart. I felt so sorry for Libya and Libyans for all those wasted years and opportunities for all that we had collectively seen and endured. My heart ached; it physically ached.

Sometimes I felt like Tom Hanks in the movie 'Cast Away', a great survival story about a man who was stranded on a deserted island for years and how hard he found it when he finally got back to civilization. I had struggled to get acclimatized to the world again, an environment complete with an endless array of choices. I felt lost. I saw how my traumatic experience had separated me from the world. It was clear to me that a part of me would still be living in war-torn Libya for the rest of my life.

I attended the retreat and spoke to my boss about coming to Tunis to work together. He welcomed the idea, so the crisis was averted. He was going to travel for a meeting, and I went back to Libya to pack up and start working from Tunis.

When I got home and told my parents, they were excited for me. It was hard to leave the school, and my students were sad. Some of them said they wouldn't come back if I weren't around. The admin team and the teachers bade me farewell with a cake and refreshments and gave me a silver necklace with my name on it. I wore that necklace whenever I needed courage or to remember who I really was and that I was a good person.

I could not see Mohamed to say goodbye, so we said it over the phone. We thought it would be easier for us to meet in Tunis than in Libya.

I rented a studio apartment a couple of minutes' walk from work, and as luck would have it, it was near the US Embassy. I brought mum to stay with me because I wanted her to see how beautiful and normal things were here. It was my gift for her, and she loved it. She went out every day. She deactivated her Whats-App, telling me she did not want any reminders of home. 'They can do without me for a couple of weeks,' she said. I would leave her money on the living room table every morning before going to work so she could do whatever she wanted. We went out to dinner at restaurants with live music, and we took long strolls on the corniche, admiring the luminous moonlight that painted the lake.

After mum went back to Libya, I decided to focus on work and improve myself. I worked from mid-October until mid-December, and my boss was very pleased with my performance. He asked me to come back and continue working from Tunis. I was more than happy to oblige, but I was glad to return home as I had missed Libya and my friends. I had breakfast at O2 with a couple of friends, but I spent most of my time with my boyfriend. I had not seen him in two months, though we talked and sent pictures all the time.

————

THE PERFECT PRESENT

I went back to Tunis in January 2017. It was very cold. Mohamed promised to come and visit for my birthday in February.

It was one cold February night when he arrived. I had dinner ready for him. We ate, chatted, and fell asleep. We decided to stay in for my birthday, so we ordered some food and watched a movie together, holding hands the entire time. We spent the whole weekend in bed under the duvet. We were in a nice place. It felt comfortable, like wearing a pair of your favourite Christmas socks. It was so nice waking up to him next to me. Nobody had to rush anywhere. There was no fear of clashes erupting, no problem with me staying out late, no chariot turning into a pumpkin. We had no history there and were far away from it all. It was incredible. He stayed a week.

My temporary relocation to Tunis could not have come at a better time. With some distance from my life in Libya, I started to see how significant the impact on me had been, living under duress for so long. How was I able to live like that? How and when did I get used to all of that? I did not know, and I could not tell.

After the initial signs of PTSD that I had exhibited when first arriving in Tunis—jumping from my seat and panicking on hearing a door slamming or thinking there was a power outage when the motion sensor light went out in the office toilet while I was daydreaming in there—I began to relax. I looked after myself. I cooked, went out for long walks, watched movies and TV series. It felt like I was on holiday. I worked hard as well, but I kept my colleagues at a distance. I did not socialize with them after work. I either went back home for my lunch break or ate at my desk. They had tried to penetrate the bubble I had around me, but eventually, they gave up.

In May, it was Ramadan, and things started to heat up in Tripoli. The brigade Mohamed belonged to was determined to get the gangs out of the area, and clashes began between the two warring parties. The fighting was intense, and it lasted a couple of weeks. Mohamed's brother decided to join the fighting, and unfortunately, he died. I heard about it through a friend of mine, Azzam, who texted me the news. He did not know we were dating, so it was more like 'the brother of so and so died in the clashes.' My heart sank into my shoes. I felt terrible for him and his parents. This was the second son. I called Mohamed, though I did not know what to say, but he made it easier. I wish I could have been there for him.

At the end of this violent round, evil was obliterated. Mohamed was able to come back home. Stability was restored. He helped the neighbours with their grievances and gave them back their properties and whatever else had been taken from them.

In August, we decided to go to Bali together. It was completely different from anything I had done before. I am used to spending my holidays in the south of France, Greece, Malta or England, Vienna or Prague, so Bali would not be my choice as it was outside my comfort zone, but I was glad to do something out of character and experience new things.

Mohamed did a lot of surfing and snorkeling. I did not, of course. We visited a lot of temples and parks and went to the zoo. The scenery was breathtaking. I loved swimming with him. I would get on his back, and he would take care of the rest, making fun of my swimming skills in the process.

We had a wonderful time. It was mesmerizing. Then I went back to Tunis, and Mohamed returned to Libya. We planned to meet in Libya in December.

———

A Reluctant Return – 2018

Many security assessments had taken place, and it was decided that the environment was now conducive to working from Libya. However, the international staff would live on a compound and under restricted movements. To that end, the office was engaged in discussions with the Regional Office and other stakeholders about lifting the evacuation status and returning to Libya.

I was not thrilled about that, as I did not want to go back. I had gotten used to my autonomy, to living on my own. I also knew that going back would mean I would have to deal with my failed marriage and end it officially.

I did not know how to introduce myself to people anymore: single, married, separated? Tunis was the perfect place for me to hide, away from the prying eyes of the neighbours and my family's unasked questions. I was scared. I hoped for the evacuation status to remain, but it did not. We were to go back in May. I savoured every moment until then.

After returning to Libya, it took me a while to re-adjust, but I focused on my work instead. It was a very busy time for us trying to operate from Tripoli. I started looking for a lawyer, and when I found one, I emailed James to let him know that I was going to have a consultation session with the lawyer to see how we could dissolve the marriage. He did not acknowledge my email.

I went ahead and booked an appointment. I canceled three times out of sheer panic before I was able to meet with her. She was a confident lady, beautiful and strong. She had photos of herself, her husband, and her son on the bookshelf behind her. I asked her to walk me through the process and asked if she could spare my family any humiliation in the process. I could not let the word get out. She gave me an alternative whereby James would divorce me in England, scan me the document, and she would register it in court. I was happy with the proposal.

I went back home and emailed him the information. He replied to me in an offhand tone saying how busy he was right now, and if he found some free time over the weekend, he would think about it. I waited for his reply for days, but it did not come. After weeks of waiting, I hired the lawyer and proceeded with the divorce on my own.

My relationship with Mohamed was great, and we went to the beach together. There was a regatta, and he took me out to the sea on a jet ski. It was exhilarating. He was supposed to go to Tunis with his friends soon, and I was to follow him at the end of August for a friend's wedding.

———

POLITICS, HENNA, AND HUSBANDS

I settled back into my old life and saw my friends when I could, but the same issues in the country persisted. I resumed my weekly visit to the Turkish bath, where I met the same girls I saw there every Saturday morning before moving to Tunis. They remembered me. One of them was married, and she always complained about how inattentive her husband was, saying that no matter how much effort she put into making herself beautiful for him, he never seemed to notice. She was very pretty, but she could not see it. She wanted to see a look on her husband's face when he looked at her. Clearly, that look was not there. I wanted to tell her that she should do these things for herself and not for her husband's approval, but then I remembered all those times I was driving around looking for a hairdresser to fix my unruly hair. Yes, I do things for myself, like being in the bath right now, and other things like meditating, eating healthy, and looking after myself, but there are other things I do for the man in my life, so maybe we are not that different after all. We were all guilty of varying degrees in that department. So I smiled and did not say anything.

I loved the bath. It was big, with changing rooms, other rooms for waxing, and a huge yard for henna. Women sat on the benches and the floor, extending their bare arms and legs to the workers there to draw henna while bonding over politics and husbands.

FOURTEEN
THE BEGINNING OF THE END

With no prior warning, some militias that belonged to a city about 60 km from Tripoli and strongly affiliated with General Haftar decided to attack the city and try to enter it. The forces already deployed in Tripoli rushed to the front line to defend the city. Rockets started falling randomly on people's houses.

That was mid-August. I thought the situation would be contained soon. Mohamed was already in Tunis with his friends, and I was getting ready to travel for Ahmed's wedding, but the fighting intensified. Many civilians were killed, children included; others injured. Mohamed asked me to change my plans and travel earlier, but I could not swing that with my boss. We were told to work from home and not move around the city. After another week, the international staff was relocated to Tunis. They traveled by road, as it was not safe to fly. Only two critical staff remained behind.

How many times can you watch your city getting destroyed? The bombardment continued, and the airport soon became the target. Rockets hit it at peak times, rendering all flights suspended. I promised my friend I would attend the wedding, but I did not know if I could fly. The airport kept on operating, as usual, closing for a few hours after each hit.

Another week went by, and I was due to travel. The night before my flight, the airport was hit repeatedly, and it shut down, but it resumed flights in the morning. My flight was the first one out, at 08:05. The airport was hit again after my plane took off, once more closing until further notice. If you are wondering how I was feeling when I was at the airport, knowing full well it was hit the previous night, if you think I might have been scared, the answer is I don't know. You get to a point where you are so emotionally overwhelmed that you cannot access your feelings anymore, and you just keep on moving.

I got to Tunis and called Mohamed, who told me he was now on his way back to Tripoli! I was shouting at the airport. I just could not believe my bad luck. He said things were getting serious, and he could not leave his comrades fighting alone. 'I have to defend my city,' he said. I was disappointed, but at least the wedding was still on.

I could not go back to Libya because the airport was still not operating. I was so tense. I could not enjoy my time there. The head of the UN mission in Libya held meetings every day with the warring parties, trying so hard to get them to agree to a ceasefire. After some weeks, they finally agreed. The airport was reopened, and I got back. The ceasefire was soon broken, and fighting started again.

Finally, after two horrible months, the war ended. The government had to settle this through financial means. They got their money, and they retreated. The office was in disarray. It was decided that a partial return of the international staff would take place in January. The city was still in panic. We just could not believe that it was all over. What if they came back?

Soon it was autumn. The air was crisp, and pomegranate and sweet potatoes were in abundance. I could smell the rain—*winter was coming!*

We welcomed 2019 with hopes and more hopes for a better Libya. Rumours were circulating that General Haftar still had his eyes on Tripoli and that he had organised an army over the years and they would now come and liberate us. Many friends and colleagues made 'Game of Thrones' jokes referencing the Army of The Dead that was coming from beyond the Wall. We were unfazed but sorely mistaken.

Around mid-March, Mohamed decided to travel with some of his friends to Europe. We said goodbye, and I continued working and following up with my lawyer on my divorce process, which was underway. All this while the army was inching its way into the outskirts of Tripoli. On the 4th of April, the clashes started in earnest. Civilians hurried indoors; brigades rushed to the frontlines. It was intense bombardment right from the get-go. The international staff that was present on the ground was evacuated yet again.

We do not even ask for happiness, just a little less pain.

— CHARLES BUKOWSKI

Thousands of people living in close proximity to the clashes had to leave their homes. Rockets fell on civilians' homes, killing children in their beds. The airport was targeted daily. The attacking side quickly gained ground and had air supremacy. Both sides took to the sky to fight each other, and airstrikes were conducted every day. It was the worst time ever. It was tragic.

Some of my colleagues became displaced due to the clashes and were looking for a place to rent. There was a time when I could not take a shower because I was so scared a rocket would join me in the bathroom. Power cuts soon followed the offensive on the capital, and the water was cut off by a tribe affiliated with the attacking side. They announced that it would remain off until the government in Tripoli allowed the army to enter. "The army is here to save you from the tyrannical rule of the militias," they said.

I plunged into despair and fear. As I was following the news to make sense of the nonsensical, I read that Mohamed's brother had been kidnapped. I contacted Mohamed, and he confirmed the sad news. He did not know his brother's whereabouts or have any lead that might take him to him. He was getting ready to come back and join the front line. I begged him not to; it was different this time. Do you remember the radar I mentioned at the beginning of the book, the one you develop over years of fear and desperation? Well, mine was perfect at that stage. This battle was not like any other. Both sides were equal in armoury, capital, and international support.

Mohamed returned at the end of April and joined the front line. Soon it was Ramadan, a time for peaceful reflection and spiritual cleansing, but that did not deter them from fighting. Many attempts from the UN to stop the fights failed. Both parties rejected ceasefires proposals.

I kept going to work, and so did my colleagues. I don't know why I didn't say I could not go and that I was anxious and had to look after my wellbeing. I was on autopilot.

I called Mohamed, who was home. I asked about his brother, but he did not have any updates. We chatted for a few minutes, and I begged him not to go. He said, "I hope everything gets better," Then we hung up.

Friday 17th of May was an ordinary day, but this would all change for me soon. After breaking the fast, I retreated to my bedroom, getting ready to sleep. I was in bed when my friend texted me. Mohamed had been hit in the clashes; he had lost a kidney and slipped into a coma. I am getting dizzy just writing this right now. I do not want to relive this, but I have to for him.

I jumped out of bed and started running around my room. I could not contain the feelings that rushed through me. I wanted to escape them. I wanted to escape from me. I called Mohamed, but his phone was off. I cried harder and more painfully than I ever had in my life. I checked the news. All the outlets were repeating the same information—he had been medevacked to Rome.

In the days that followed the awful news, I tried to find out anything I could about him. I kept checking the internet for news, checking his WhatsApp status every few minutes, and calling his number, even though I knew it was off. I was going in circles in my room like a wounded lion in a cage. There was no escape.

I kept texting Azzam, who had told me the news, just to see if he had heard anything. He was naturally curious about Mohamed, and as luck would have it, he had a friend in Rome, so he got in touch with him for an update. He did not know that we were together, and that was not the time for me to explain what my heart wanted.

I lived and died every day, many times. I started by checking his WhatsApp online status, checking the news, texting my friend, and listening to Mohamed's voice by playing the WhatsApp voice messages. I could not focus on my job anymore. I wanted to travel to Tunis so that I could fly to Rome from there. I wanted to give him my kidney. He had my heart already, so what was a kidney? I asked my boss to let me travel, and he refused.

I began to unravel slowly. I started making a lot of mistakes, getting into fights with my boss, forgetting things. One day, I was in my office alone, and the door was closed. I was looking online for some news and started crying. A colleague entered the office and saw me in tears. She felt awkward. She asked, 'are you okay?' I just said, "Yes, I am. What can I do for you?" It was very awkward. The poor girl did not know what to do or what to say.

I was like a glass on a rickety table full to its brim with water. I was in pain; my body was in pain. I would wake up in the morning, and my body would refuse to move. I dragged myself out of my bed to the shower. Even driving felt like a huge deal; it felt like the car was on my back. I cannot count the times I had to pull over to the side of the road and burst into tears just because I could not go on anymore.

I spoke to my boss again about letting me work from Tunis, and he refused again. We had a high-level visit from HQ, and after that, he was going to Tunis. He said I could travel then, so I was forced to carry on just a little longer.

I was involved in the preparations for the visit, and one day, the delegation was supposed to have dinner with key staff and stakeholders. I collapsed on a chair in the office and started crying. My head was dizzy, and I could not breathe. My colleagues thought I was having an anxiety attack. I did not know what that was; I just knew I wanted my love to wake up and feel better.

My friend checked with his friend in Rome, who told him Mohamed was still in a coma. He was one kidney down, and parts of his liver had been removed. He was on a ventilating machine because his lungs were also damaged.

All of our beautiful moments seemed so far away. I tried to hang on to them, but they were slipping away. I was in the middle of a raging war, trying to find out anything, any updates on his state. I hated those days. I was trying to travel, and the airport kept being hit by rockets day and night.

In the middle of all of this, my lawyer called. My case was up, and she wanted me to supply her with the names of witnesses so she could book the judge. She wanted those names NOW. The witnesses were to appear before the judge to corroborate my story so that he could grant me a divorce. I had tried to think about who could do that over the years, wanting to spare my family the experience. I told my lawyer to give me a few minutes, and I would call her back. She said I should call her soon. Otherwise, the judge would move on, at which point we would have to wait for months since judges were getting ready for their sabbatical.

I asked if I could use friends. I would not ask a friend to do that, but I just wanted to know the options. She advised against it. She said it would be better to bring a family member, as they were the ones who knew the story. Well, they did not know what had happened. I had been backed into a corner.

I gave them the names of my mother, my brother, and my sister. Then I called my sister and explained. They had to stand before the judge tomorrow morning. My sister said she would do it; she just needed me to give her the wedding date since she was hazy on the details. I called my mother, but she started yelling down the line. She said, "absolutely not!" I begged her. She said we would talk when I got home after work.

I got home to find there was no electricity again, and for the first time ever, I was grateful for the timing of the power cuts: at least I could hide my face, and I would not have to see my mother's angry face and disappointment. I spoke to my sister first, then my brother. They were both cooperative and matter-of-fact. Then I went downstairs to my mother. Her dim figure was looking away. I begged her to do this for me. This was my only chance of getting back my freedom and correcting my mistake. I also told her that I had no other choice; it had to be the family. I reassured her that they would just have to go into a room with the judge and answer some questions. The judge only wanted confirmation of the time spent apart, which was the grounds for the divorce.

She said, "I never believed that I would do that for my daughter." Strange, living with them with my current status was okay, but somehow getting that fixed was an issue for her. My sister was able to convince my mother to go with them to the judge the following day. I was relieved—one less thing to worry about now.

———

I do not know how many times I broke down in tears when I thought about Mohamed lying alone on a hospital bed. I hoped against hope that he would wake up. I was desperate. There was nothing I could have done. All I had was his number, which had been off since mid-May. I left him many WhatsApp voice messages to find when he woke up. Some of those messages made it into his inbox, where I told him how much I loved him and reminded him of some funny moments and the first time we swapped numbers, while others I had deleted as they did not make much sense. I was consumed with sadness, so I just babbled on and on. It was a way to reach out to him to stay connected to him.

I was scheduled to travel on June 27, after the delegation visit. I wanted to see what could be done. I could go to Rome from Tunis; I could not do anything from here. My best friend, the one I had met at the French Institute, was also to travel to Tunis on the same day. He was going to Germany to visit his brother, so we agreed to meet on the 27th for dinner since he was leaving the next day.

The next day brother drove me to the airport. When he left, I realised I had left my passport at home. I called my brother and told him, then waited for him to return with my passport. My brain had failed me. My passport was only one of a series of things I had forgotten. My performance at work had declined further as well. I was reeling.

I got to Tunis; my best friend and I were to meet in the evening. I continued my attempts to find any updates, then went out in the evening and met with my friend. He had made the reservation under my boyfriend's first name and the last name of a girl he had loved very much, though it had not been reciprocated. He said the dinner was to honour the two people who had had the most profound impact on us. It was very poetic. I loved the gesture.

After dinner, my friend and I went for a walk along the coastal road and then went down to the beach. We took off our shoes and felt the cold sand between our toes, then sat on the sand, close enough for the waves to kiss the tips of our toes. We spoke a lot about love, and he asked me if my man was the love of my life." Yes," I said," without a shadow of a doubt." I talked a lot about him, what made me love him so much, and how I would never feel the same about anybody else. He told me that he would wake up and recover and that I would be able to say all of those things and more to him, face to face.

We got up and walked back to the coast road. We were to go our separate ways now. We hugged and kissed. I wished him a great time with his brother, and he told me to text him the minute Mohamed woke up from his coma.

I got into a taxi and waved goodbye.

FIFTEEN
THE DARKEST HOUR

F riday, June 28, 2019, started as an ordinary day. I went to the bank, then met my friend, the one whose wedding I had attended back in 2018. We had breakfast together. He said his wife was expecting, and he was very happy; he showed me an app he had on his phone to track the pregnancy term and the development of the baby. I was happy for them both. I finished my breakfast and went home.

Around 16:00, I went to bed to lie down for a bit, but I received a text message from my friend, Azzam, telling me that my boyfriend had passed on.

For a few seconds, I sat on the bed, feeling empty. I did not know how to respond. I texted: "Really? Are you sure?" He said yes, "it is all over the news. He died this morning."

I dashed to the living room, typed his name in, and there he was, pictures and pictures of him. I knew each and every single facial expression in those photos. There was no expression that was strange to me. I knew what he was feeling in each of those photos.

He had remained in a coma for forty-two days before he

finally slipped away. I cried and cried. I could not believe he was gone.

Social media were full of messages from mourners: people he had helped, friends, comrades. Everybody was in utter shock. I did not want to live anymore. I was in so much pain there were no words to describe how I felt. A whole era of my life had been erased. I felt hopeless and bereft. I could not believe that this was it; this was the end—the end of our story. There would be no more him, no more us. I would never see him again, never touch him again, never kiss him again.

I could not move, I could not work, I could not do anything. My grief came in waves. I would drown in it for a bit. Then for a while, I would be silent.

While the internet was buzzing with him and his heroic stories, there was nothing about the funeral. I started to get agitated. I wanted to know when he would be brought back to Libya. In those days, my imagination got the better of me. I started imagining that maybe the doctors had made a mistake and found out that he was still alive, which was why he had not been brought back to Libya. I kept following the narrative and then caught myself halfway and forced myself back to reality. The narrative I was weaving sounded so much better than my reality.

It was six days before they announced his burial date: July 4th. I could not stay home. I wanted to escape the news. I texted my friend and colleague, Roza, whom I occasionally confided in about my relationship, and told her he would be buried tomorrow. She asked me. "Do you know where they will bury him?" I replied, "In my heart." I went to the beach, sat there, and cried my heart out. I was in pieces.

My boss sent me a message asking me if I could stay and work from Tunis, but I could not be around people. I was not able to compose myself. I was shattered, so I asked to work from home for a time before returning to Libya.

I went back to Libya around the third week of July and returned to work. My leave was due at the beginning of August, and I thought I would keep it together until then. I stayed at my desk, worked, and went home, where I cried and slept.

One day, I decided to drive down the alley where I had met Mohamed, the one where we used to meet. I drove a little bit, then stopped in the middle. I started shaking. I turned the car around, and I drove back home. I could not go through with it.

Mohamed was everywhere in my room: things I had bought for our dates, things I had worn for special dates. I had a story for us in every song. He had been with me, living in me for years. Now he was no longer there. I did not make sense without him.

Finally, it was time for me to go on leave. I put away my laptop and decided to give in and collapse. I had been holding on since May, and now I would let go. The first day was okay, but on the second day, I got sick. At first, I thought I was coming down with a cold, and I did not care, but the symptoms persisted and got worse. I had pain in my chest and would cough all day long. My body could not move anymore. I was bedridden for days.

Finally, my brother took me to the clinic, and it turned out I had severe pneumonia. I was hospitalized. My stomach could not keep anything down, including medicines. I stayed for over a week before I was released. I went back home feeling as sick as I had been when I had left it. It was painful to move, painful to breathe. All that stress had finally caught up with me. There was a time when I vomited in my room or on the way to the toilet, as I was in so much pain that I could not move quickly. Soon my brother got me a bucket to put near my bedside.

I remained unwell for five weeks, and then at the beginning of September, I started to walk and move with little or no pain. I went back to work but took it easy. I was afraid to eat in case I vomited, so I was careful with my food and medicine. I still coughed occasionally, but in no way like before. I was on the mend, slowly. By the end of September, I was out of the woods.

At the end of September, the judge granted me my divorce. As for the war, it raged on; no side had the upper hand. The airport was no longer operational because of all the damage from the shelling. Mohamed's brother was still missing, and nobody knew if he was dead or alive.

I missed Mohamed unfathomably. I cried every night, every single night. When you love someone so much, and they die, you are left with so much love and nowhere for this love to go. It is like a car crashing into a wall. He was my person, the other sock in a pair. He was so sweet and tender with me. Whenever I was weary or sad, I would call him, and the minute I said "hello," he would say right away, "what's wrong?" He knew me. I was understood. He was my security blanket.

I am so lonely without him. If I could see him just one last time, even in a dream—just once. I thought about all the days, the months ahead of me without him. The New Year, the birthdays, the summers without him. How would I go through it all without him? I could not and did not want to. I caught myself having many imaginary conversations with him, about my mundane existence, about work, just normal stuff, then I would jolt myself out of it. I felt sorry for myself. I woke up with a heavy heart every morning and a tingling sensation in my stomach—a bad one. I hated waking up and feeling that way, but there was nothing to do about it.

I could not visit Mohamed's resting place. I could not do it. The very few people who knew about the relationship advised me to go and visit the grave to accept what had happened, but I was not in denial; I knew he was gone. I just was not strong enough to go there. Maybe in the future, but right then, I was not able to. I put all the clothes I used to wear when I was with him in a bag and threw them away. I did not see the point in keeping them: he was gone.

I started thinking about 2019; how much it had taken from me, the misery, the displaced people, the children who had died. We were all prisoners of war.

Pneumonia left me frail. Looking back on my sickness now, I am relieved it was prior to Covid-19. Otherwise, I would have thought I had caught the virus. After much reflection, I decided to challenge 2019 and end it on a positive note. I decided to go to London. I booked my accommodation in Paddington and made sure it was non-refundable. I was daring fate. I booked a ticket to my favourite musical, *The Phantom of the Opera*.

I had to plan my way out of Tripoli. With no airport, a city that is 200km from Tripoli started operating flights instead of our tiny airport. That was my route. I decided to go at the end of November and stay two weeks in Tunis and then to London. I could not wait until the last minute in Tripoli as the clashes were getting closer every day. I was worried my route would be cut off.

I booked my ticket and a hired driver from the agency to drive me. The road was not 100% safe, as there were checkpoints, and some were affiliated with the side trying to take over Tripoli. Many travelers were robbed on their way to the airport. I kept my cash and cards in my socks.

The driver picked me up in the morning. He got us some cappuccino and sandwiches, put some music on, and we took off. We kept running into checkpoints. Before we approached one of them, he would switch off the music until we drove past them. They all ushered us through. Nobody stopped us. Some of them had black masks on; those were the scariest ones. I was too scared to breathe. I held my breath until we passed a checkpoint.

The driver finally dropped me off at the airport, I paid him, and he left. My colleagues and brother kept texting and calling all the way to check on me. The trip was risky but necessary. It was a long day, and I arrived in Tunis at night. I was safe, where no rockets could reach me.

London, here I come.

Sixteen

London

I spent my days in Tunis working and thinking about London and what I would do there. I almost dissolved with excitement. But after a few days, I fell ill with a bad cold and a fever and had to stay in bed for a week. I was too sick to go out and see a doctor or a pharmacist. It was really bad. It was clear to me that all the duress had compromised my immune system.

But I recovered, and the anticipated day of my travel was finally here. I got up early in the morning, had breakfast, showered, and dressed up. I was ready for London.

When a man is tired of London, he is tired of life; for there is in London all that life can afford.

— Samuel Johnson

A REUNION

I arrived at Heathrow in the evening and went to WH Smith for a SIM card and snacks for the night. I got into a taxi, and we drove off. It was drizzling. I was there, finally. It was dark, but I looked out of the window, wanting to take everything in. I let myself into my accommodation and settled in.

When I woke up very early the next morning, I felt paralysed. I could not go out. I was suddenly overwhelmed by the immensity of the city. I did not know where to start and what to do. I did not know how to unwind. I grabbed my phone and looked at Google Maps to see my surroundings. I was hungry and needed to eat, but I was scared to leave. I looked for any place that offered breakfast and found a hotel behind my place. I used the directions, and I was there in less than two minutes. I had breakfast, and I felt good.

I went back to my room and stayed there. I decided I needed a crash course on the London Underground. I re-familiarised myself with the system and watched videos on how to get and top-up an Oyster card. I had been far from this environment for so long that I couldn't remember how to get into it again.

I stayed home that day and just went to the local shops for groceries and bought shortbread. I love shortbread.

I woke up the next day feeling a little less tense. I had breakfast at the same place I had gone to the previous day: I am a creature of habit. I went to Paddington Station, and I asked where I could get an Oyster card. I followed the directions and found the machines. I wanted a machine with no queue behind me, as queues always made me nervous. I hate making people wait, and I really needed time to figure out this machine card thing. It had been a few years since I had been in London. The war had put blinkers on my head like a horse. I had been thinking about only one thing for years—surviving. All the other things had disappeared. I went for a cash machine and not credit cards, as everybody was queuing to pay with their cards. I inserted the cash and got my Oyster. It felt like an accomplishment. War does change people. It takes away their best parts.

I chose the line, and just like that—I was on the train. It was like riding a bicycle, never forgotten. I went everywhere: Notting Hill, Piccadilly, Oxford, Edgeware Road, Buckingham Palace, Westminster, the River Thames. I went to China Town and Waterstone's. I went to Winter Wonderland and played like a child. I did not follow Google Maps anymore; I didn't need to. I had a plan every day, and it felt wonderful. I went to the cinema and saw a lot of movies. With each passing day, I felt more like a human being. Sometimes I would just wake up and go out, letting the streets take me anywhere. I left shopping until my last week. I wanted to enjoy the city first and just walk and walk and walk. I felt so good.

I loved the Christmas festivities. The lights, the decorations, the window display of Selfridges. It warmed my heart. Santa was proud, for sure. The only thing I had struggled with was eating out. I was always seated at the bar; tables were for couples. I was often seated with families or friends to play certain games or ride the Ferris Wheel at Winter Wonderland. I was embarrassed, but hey—I was there.

London was a melting pot, full of people from all walks of life. I did not feel uncomfortable. I did not stand out—and if I am being honest, I would not have cared if I had. It is ironic how sometimes the thing you fight is actually yourself. When I was walking around, I realised that perhaps I had not been open enough to people all those years when I was living here, and that was why I had felt out of place. I did not show them who I really was. I was too busy fighting all of those labels, the 'otherness' that was pinned on me. It almost felt like I was buried under them. In not wanting to be defined by them, I lost sight of very important things: to breathe, let go, and not be inside my head the whole time.

Here I was, after everything, despite everything, I was back in London, ending the year on a great note.

I carry your heart with me, I carry it in my heart.

— E.E. CUMMINGS

As I walked around the streets of London, I thought of the love of my life and how nice it would have been if we were together, or If I could just video call him and we could chat. I walked past several nice clothing stores for men and felt a pain in my stomach. Sadly, I realised I could not buy anything for him anymore—no scarves, no hats, no watches, no nice sweaters. Nobody was eagerly waiting for me to come back either. My loneliness was palpable, but I would always carry him in my heart.

A New Year and a New Start

I booked an appointment at a hair salon in Edgeware Road to dye my hair. I dyed it dark brown, my natural colour—I just wanted to accentuate it. The salon was so good I decided to go back and get a blow-dry for the New Year.

On the morning of the 31st of December, I woke up with a smile. I checked my phone and found a number of voice messages from colleagues and friends wishing me the best for the New Year. It felt like it was my birthday.

I went out. It was drizzling again. I went to the hairdresser's first, then walked along the River Thames in my raincoat, all the while reflecting on the whole year, how much pain I had endured, the losses, the uncertainties. Most importantly, I thought about healing and coming out from the darkest recesses of my mind. I did not know what lay ahead on my journey to healing myself, but I knew it would take time. I also thought about hope and coping mechanisms under duress and how much inner strength they could give you, but they can also isolate you. When each day becomes solely about survival, you miss a lot—you change and lose some parts of yourself. I knew I had to cast off my own proverbial prison and try to find hope and healing among the wreckage of my heart.

I went to Café Nero and had a big cup of hot chocolate with cream on top. I sat there and savoured it. Then I went back home to get changed and get ready for the evening.

I wore a nice black tutu dress and went out. I could not get a place at a restaurant for just one, and to be honest, I did not want to stay indoors. I wanted to go out and feel everything. I wanted everything to touch me: people, raindrops, wind. I wanted to feel alive.

After walking around Oxford Street and Piccadilly, I decided to head to Covent Garden. I walked around the market there and then got a little tired, so I sat down on one of the benches there. A few minutes later, I was approached by a man who must have been in his late forties. He leaned forward and said gently," Can I join you?" I was going to be sitting there for a while before going back to Oxford Street for the fireworks, so I invited him to sit down. He sat down and immediately commented on the weather. "It's so cold," he said. I agreed. Then he looked at me, registering my features, and asked inquisitively, " Where are you from" I looked at him, wondering how I would get out of this one. I told him to guess. He smiled and said, 'Spain?'

"No."

"Greece?"

"No." I looked into his blue eyes and said, "Libya."

His face was blank. He was trying to come up with a reaction but failed. I looked back at him. I smiled and said: "You don't know where Libya is, do you?" He did not. He was embarrassed not to know, but it didn't matter. It didn't bother me. I explained where Libya was on the map, and he recognized the area. We chatted for a bit. He offered to go with me to eat somewhere, but I politely declined. I did not want anybody to take this night away from me. I had come all the way from Libya for this. I wished him a happy New Year, and we parted ways.

THE COUNTDOWN

I made my way back to Oxford Street and the surrounding areas. People were heading towards a big square to watch the fireworks, and I joined them. I found myself a perfect spot where I was surrounded by families, couples, and friends. I was the only one on my own, but I was not lonely. It was fine. I was touched by the collective experience. I am an empath if you have not figured that out about me by now. I felt the love that was there, the hope, the dreams, the anticipation. I stood there, and I took it all in.

As the clock ticked its hands towards twelve, many people took their phones out and started taking selfies. Others made video calls to their loved ones and families. I looked around at them, wondering about the stories everybody was living—the highs and the lows. Well, it did not matter; everybody was there to start anew, and I was a part of that.

We all joyfully started counting, 10, 9, 8, 7, 6, 5, 4, 3, 2, 1... It was the final countdown.

Happy New Year!

To a beautiful soul
    Thanks for the memories

— SARA LEPTIS

Epilogue

S

o, after 14 months (April 2019 – June 2020), the raging war on Tripoli had ended—a tragedy that unfolded at a staggering speed and scale. Haftar and his troops failed to enter Tripoli. They retreated, and I could not believe it when I heard the news. I woke up every day slowly, anticipating and waiting for that sound. The sound of bombardment that had accompanied me for 14 months, but there was nothing. It was all quiet—no more clashes. The calmness felt unfamiliar. I was relieved, do not get me wrong. But I just could not immediately identify with this "normal" state.

Also, I could not let myself be happy and enjoy it—what if they were on a break or a truce? What if they were still loitering on the outskirts of Tripoli. I could not afford another disappointment. It was like I had been kidnapped for far too long, and one day my kidnapper left the door unlocked by mistake, but I could not break free. So, I waited. After a few days, the news of their retreat had been confirmed, and only then I permitted myself to feel relieved. I cried. It was a different kind of crying. A different kind of tears. How can I put this? They were tears of relief as the war – or at least this war – was behind us now. They were tears of guilt as I was alive, my family's home was intact, but many Libyans lost their homes. They had to evacuate as they were right in the conflict-affected areas. Some were able to go back to a partially intact home; others to ransacked houses, completely damaged houses, or houses with planted bombs and explosives. They were tears of fear as I did not know when this black cloud would descend on us again. It is still hovering over our heads, threatening to shower us with its angry thunderstorm and drown us in blood baths one more time. They were tears of gratitude for the lives of all those who died defending my city and all those innocent ones who died in the safety of their homes by an angry missile. My tears tasted differently than they used to.

It is almost two years now since Mohamed has passed and a year since I wrote this book. A lot has passed and happened, and the world as we all know it has changed. Do you think I will ever find love again? Do you think I have found love? Maybe this is a story for another book.

Am I happy? What do you think become of my broken heart? You know when they say, "Take each day as it comes and one day at a time," I could not relate to that before. I thought it was a cliché to make our life better, put a temporary band-aid on a wound, but I was wrong. This is what I did. I took each day as it came—less actually. I took one part of the day as it came, and I stopped myself from getting overwhelmed by thinking ahead.

It was equally challenging to think about Mohamed and not think about him. I had a lot of memories—funny ones, warm and loving ones, silly ones. It was painful to reminisce, but it was also difficult to keep playing those memories in my head over and over again. I was afraid I would wear them out. They were like a favourite jacket, a pair of shoes, or a dress. If you keep wearing it, you will ruin it eventually. But how can you stop yourself from wearing your favourite article of clothing? I was afraid to forget one of them, afraid that one of those memories would escape my sad and stressed mind and leave me all alone in despair. They were too many, but they were finite. I won't get to make any more memories with him. I won't get to do anything with him again. I often caught myself making new memories, fake ones with him, where we are both happy and together—me doting on him, playing with his hair, linking my fingers with his. What I have is all I was ever going to get. So, my loss was multi-layered. It was not only that he was gone; it was what his loss represented to me and how it manifested itself in my life.

However, this is what happened to me, and this is how I saw my life; in chapters—the before and after the loss. What followed after December, 2019 was irrelevant to my story and who I was back then. 2020 was the chapter of COVID-19 and everything new it brought with it. It was social distancing and quarantining and baking bread. All of that was not and could not be part of my story. It did not make sense to me to include anything after December, 2019 as that part of my life ended right there and then, and I chose London to close that chapter as some things do come full circle. It started with me in England, feeling out of place, uncertain feelings about returning to Libya to coming back to London to end that era there. I came back to London not feeling out of place, but rather feeling okay even if I did. It did not matter in the grand scheme of things. I learned that it was okay to stand out, and let me tell you, around Christmas time in London, nobody can stand out. It is just not possible. It felt right to go back to where everything started and end that era there. Everything that followed after that is different. I was different because of everything that happened to me, all the losses I had suffered, the heartbreak, the wars—simply everything.

Libya and I are still picking up the pieces, trying to make

sense of it all and move on. Neither has gotten their happy ending.

Libya continues to be in turmoil but having a temporary lull from the wars, while I remind myself to enjoy every "normal" day as we get very few of them, and the rest...well, I will deal with it when I get there.

I am different. Some parts of me do not quite fit in the same place as they used to. I do not go out much, as most streets are dotted with our memories, like the cherry blossom trees shedding their flowers on the ground of a park—they are everywhere, they penetrate your senses. You see them, you smell them, and you touch them, you cannot escape. I guess that is the beauty and the pain of having so many memories and living in a war zone.

I visited his grave once. I never thought I would visit him. I do know why I did not go and why I decided to eventually. Some people thought it would make it easier for me to go and see his grave as a way of helping me face reality and move on. But I knew my reality quite well. I was not in denial about it. I just knew that he was gone, and the grave would not bring me any relief or comfort. Yet, one day I was crying, and I knew at that moment that I wanted to visit his grave. I cannot quite articulate or explain how I felt, but I knew with certainty that this was what I needed and wanted to do.

I called his sister to give me the exact location of his resting place. I went. The graveyard was not far from my house. I entered and turned right and kept on walking. The grave would be on my right with his name on the tombstone, not far away from the gate. That is what his sister said. I followed her instruction, and there it was. A new grave next to a woman who died in 1997. How sad! I thought about all the things she had missed.

I approached the grave carefully, slowly as not to awaken him, like I did many times when he slept by my side, and I wanted to sneak out to the toilet or to have a sip of water. I would walk on my toes to not wake him. I looked at the name and the date, and I sat down. I got down on my knees, touched the grave, and kissed it many times over. I did not care about the little insects that were crawling all over the grave and all around it. I talked to him, whispered a few words, and sat there quietly. I was the only one there. I looked at the grave next to him and tried to imagine what it would be like to be so dead and for this long. I thought about her family, her age, cause of death, and all she had missed. I felt sad. I got up and left. I got into my car, and I burst into tears. His sister called me to ensure I had found the place, and I thanked her in between my sobs and blocked nose. She started crying as well. She prayed that he would find peace. I echoed her sentiment, and I hung up. I drove home, got into my room, collapsed into a heap, and finished crying.

I do not really know if I will fall in love in that same way again or ever. F. Scott Fitzgerald said, "There are all kinds of love in this world, but never the same love twice." I just knew that I had to keep moving on and living.

Sometimes he crosses my mind, and I feel him so far away from me, and the me back then feels so foreign to me. It is like I have never been that version of myself, and the story never took place. I cannot imagine me sneaking out of my house to meet a guy or that I would stay awake all night waiting for a guy to call me. I am not that person anymore—I outgrew her, or she died; either way, I feel different.

Grief is consuming and multi-layered. It is laced with guilt; fear, and it is borderline insanity. You lose part of yourself, and you are never the same.

I hope my experience will resonate with many people. I at least hope they can understand.

Grief is not something you can finish and be done with. I

thought it was something to be completed, and then I can say, look, I did it: I finished grieving. In my experience, I learned that grief is a continuous and ongoing journey. It is more pronounced at times and recedes into the background at other times. All you have to do is to keep breathing and remind yourself that it will get better.

Since now I am the primary keeper of those memories, I wanted to find a way to put all my memories and stories in a time capsule, and I believe this book has helped me do it. It is my way of documenting an era and honoring a love that stood the test of time. It was like catching fireflies in a jar and putting them on your mantelpiece.

I wish I could have written more about the late Chris Stevens and how much I had loved and admired him, but I could not. It was really painful for me to revisit Chris, and I also did not want to veer off from the main story of the book. Chris could have stolen the focus of the book the way he did whenever he walked into a place. It would have been so easy to just write and write about him and the embassy – a time I still considered the happiest I had ever been. But it would have been like Cinderella at the ball where she would have to return home, to her grim reality, or her carriage would turn into a pumpkin.

As I see them, Libyans are prisoners of geography and victims of history. I catch myself thinking about an alternate reality, where we were never a pariah, where we could travel freely and easily, where we live in a world where mothers do not fear for the lives of their children or that they might get kidnapped on the way to school for ransom. How I wished things would have been different for us.

I still dream and hope for a better Libya for all those children. I hope that they will live in a peaceful and prosperous Libya. I do hope that the lives of those who died would amount to some-thing – no matter where we stand politically.

Well, my jar of fireflies is full now, and I hope it illuminates my way, moving forward with my life.

To a beautiful soul
May you rest in peace.

Acknowledgments

I would love to thank Publish Authority and Frank Eastland for making me feel like part of the Publish Authority's family. I am grateful for his guidance, patience, and kindness. I went through ups and downs when trying to finalize the book, and that was primarily due to my reluctance to re-read what I had written, as I did not want to go down that journey again. Frank was very patient with me and waited for me to be ready.

So, thank you, Frank.

ABOUT THE AUTHOR

When I was a child, I had trouble sleeping. I was scared of the nighttime and the sense of finality it brought with it. My parents enforced a strict bedtime ritual: my older sister and I would turn in exactly the same time each night. My sister was a fast sleeper. I used to beg her to stay up and tell me stories to ease my anxiety and help me fall asleep. She did her best, but being fast to fall asleep, she just could not stay awake with me. Lying awake in the dark, feeling scared and alone, I started telling myself stories to help me sleep—weaving storylines on a tapestry was something I enjoyed doing, and it has stayed with me ever since.

So, I am trying to say that I have always had stories in my head, writing themselves, but I have never seen myself as a writer. Writing happened when I was in so much pain it came pouring out of me.

I wish I were able to have my debut book under my real name. However, due to the personal story and its intimate details, I thought it was wise to write it under a nom de plume (Sara Leptis) Sara because it is an easy and a universal name, not like mine that often gave me trouble when I lived in Europe. As for "Leptis," I wanted something Libyan as the story is about Libya. Leptis is the name of a Libyan city under the Roman Empire. The city still exists to date and is a major tourist attraction.